X

Freelance

Proofreading

and

Copy-editing

A Guide

by

Trevor Horwood

ActionPrint Press

Freelance Proofreading and Copy-editing – a guide
Trevor Horwood

Published by ActionPrint Press, Virginstow, Devon EX21 5DY

British Library Cataloguing in Publication Data

A catalogue record for this book is available from the British Library

Typeset by SJ Design and Publishing, Bromley, Kent
Printed by Repro City Limited, London

ISBN 0 9523974 7 1

Contents

For Sue, without whom . . .

Introduction

Congratulations! In obtaining this guide you have taken the first step on the road to your new career as a freelance proofreader/copy-editor. The information contained here will provide you with the basic knowledge necessary to approach publishers with confidence and to complete straightforward proofreading assignments correctly and professionally.

Those without a publishing background will find the opening sections invaluable, providing as they do an insight into the world of publishing and explaining clearly the publishers' jargon which you will encounter.

There follow some instructive sections from which you will learn the basics of proofreading and copy-editing. We also touch briefly on the use of computers and other freelance opportunities which may whet your appetite.

By now you'll be eager to learn more, and we point you in the right direction by giving details of relevant societies, associations, training options and essential reference works.

The longest and most important section, Getting Started, provides you with step-by-step instructions on approaching publishers and other potential clients. We also provide a list of 101 potential customers for your new-found skills.

The text continues with a few of the financial implications of becoming self-employed and Appendices 1 to 3 contain useful listings of proofreading symbols, common errors and contact addresses. Appendix 4 comprises a series of exercises to hone your proofreading skills and to help you put into practice what you have learnt.

The book concludes with a useful glossary, bibliography and index for ease of reference.

We hope that you will enjoy reading this guide and find it a useful springboard to a new and rewarding lifestyle.

Internet Update Service

Post-publication updates to contact-list information etc. are available on the Internet at www.copyediting.co.uk.

Proper words in proper places,
make the true definition of style.

JONATHAN SWIFT

1 – Book Production

In order to understand how the work of the freelance copy-editor and proofreader fits into the overall scheme of things, we must first take a simplified look at how a book progresses from author to bookshop.

As we will see later, most publishers specialize in certain subject areas, so the author of a book on, say, flower arranging, will try to place it with a publisher that lists Arts and Crafts among their specialisms.

Such a **manuscript** (or **typescript**) will usually be considered by a **commissioning editor**. If it is accepted for publication, the commissioning editor (or perhaps another in-house editor) will be responsible for overseeing the progress of the book through its various stages of production.

At this initial stage, the commissioning editor may ask the author to rewrite certain sections or to supply more (or less) information, arrange for the provision of any necessary photographs or illustrations, and will make certain general decisions regarding the overall style of the finished book, the proposed price, how many pages it will have, how many copies to print and so on.

Once these decisions have been taken, the typescript is ready for copy-editing. A very small publisher may have to carry out these editing functions in-house for reasons of economy while a very large publisher may have sufficient resources and turnover to employ specialist staff to carry out the work on the premises. Many publishers, however, will have neither the time nor, perhaps, the specialist skills and knowledge to keep the job in the family and so will contract out the editing stage to a freelance copy-editor.

The commissioning editor may either contact the freelance directly or delegate this responsibility to another member of staff.

Once copy-edited, the typescript will be sent for **typesetting** – usually to a specialist typesetting company. The days of 'hot metal' printing, where each piece of type was inserted by hand, are long gone and today's typesetting is nearly all done via a computer keyboard.

The typesetter produces a loose-leaf print-out or **proof copy** of the book. If the book's layout is fairly complex with many illustrations (such as our hypothetical flower-arranging example above), these will probably be **galley proofs** (proofs that have not been sectioned into pages). These will be passed to a **designer** who will physically cut up the text and paste it on to a card layout, also known as a **paste-up**, leaving spaces for the illustrations etc. (This stage may also be carried out using a computer.) The paste-up will then go back to the typesetter who uses it to produce a set of **page proofs** with the text placed correctly on each loose-leaf page. A less-complex book such as a novel or a textbook would probably go straight to the page proof stage.

Page proofs will be numbered as they are to appear in the finished book. In printing terms, page numbers are known as **folios**, for instance the folio on this page is 8. (Confusingly, typescript pages themselves are also known as folios – see page 15.) Galley proofs will not contain folios, although they may have some sort of computer reference containing a number in one corner. You should have no trouble distinguishing the two types of proof.

Be they galleys or pages, the proofs will be read by a specialist proofreader – again, very often a freelance – who will ensure that no mistakes have been left in by the copy-editor or introduced by the typesetter. The author will also receive a set of proofs to check. Both sets of proofs will be returned to the publisher who will **collate** them, transferring the author's corrections on to the proofreader's set. This becomes known as the **marked set** of proofs.

Unless there are very few corrections, the marked set will be returned to the typesetter for amendment – this amended set being known as the **revise proofs**. The index (if there is one) is also usually set at this stage.

The revises will be checked, probably in-house, to ensure that all the amendments have been made correctly. The book will then be **passed for press** and the typeset manuscript sent to the printer's. A jacket will be added, advance copies produced for review, and finally a full production run printed for distribution in the market place.

This is necessarily a simplified account, and the practice of some publishers may vary slightly from it – for instance the copy-editor may be asked to collate the proofs or a colour-proof stage may be added for a book printed in full colour – but as you can see, freelance labour has a vital role to play in book production. This guide will explain how you can find your way into this large and lucrative market.

2 – Parts of a Book

Any book, and so any typescript, comprises many parts and you will need to be familiar with them all to proofread or copy-edit correctly.

A novel is perhaps the type of book with which you are most familiar at the moment, so let's start there. As an exercise in observation, take any work of fiction from your bookshelf and, before reading on, make a list of all the different parts in it that would need to be checked before publication (apart from the words comprising the story itself). Do this now before reading any further.

How did you get on? It's surprising just how complex a seemingly simple book is when examined closely. Not all of the following items are found in every book – but each one is found in many.

First, the book has a front cover (if a paperback) or a jacket (if in hardback), upon which will be printed the title and the author's name. On opening the book we often find a summary of the story, or perhaps a brief passage from it, on the first right-hand or **recto** page. (If the book has a jacket this may be printed on the front flap, or flyleaf, when it is known as the **front flap copy**.) This first page is known as the **quarter-title** page and the words (or **copy**) there is the quarter-title **blurb**.

The other side of the quarter-title page – the quarter-title **verso** – may be blank or may contain some other material such as a list of books by the same author. The recto opposite may contain the book's title only (**half-title** page) or the title and the author's name (**title** page). Not every book has a quarter- and half-title page, but you will always find a title page.

The title page also usually contains the publisher's name, sometimes their address, and probably their logo (or **colophon**, to give it its correct name). The title verso is where the full name and address of the publisher is found together with the date of publication, copyright notice, International Standard Book Number (**ISBN**) and the British Library Cataloguing in Publication (**CIP**) data. Collectively, the information found here is known as the **imprints**, and the title verso as the **imprints page**. Following the imprints page may be a **contents** list, a **dedication** or **epigraph**, some **acknowledgements**, a **foreword** (which is usually written by someone other than the author) and/or a **preface** (which is usually written by the author).

Everything found before the first page of Chapter 1 constitutes the **preliminary pages**, known as the **prelims** in publishing jargon.

You may have noticed that in some books the preliminary pages are numbered using roman numerals, i, ii, iii, etc., with arabic pagination (1, 2, 3) commencing at the first page of the text (i.e. from Chapter 1 onwards). This is so that if, for example, an author decided to insert an amended preface to a subsequent edition, only the prelims would require repagination; the text could remain unaltered.

Having negotiated the prelims, what else did you spot? Most books are divided into chapters, so you will need to check that every **chapter head** is printed in the same typeface (not **Chapter One**, Chapter Two, *Chapter Three*); and uses the same capitalization (not Chapter One, Chapter two, CHAPTER Three); and uses words or numbers consistently (not Chapter 1, 2, Chapter Three). Does each chapter title page have a number (or not as the case may be)? The book may be divided into parts by **part title** pages or the chapters may be divided into sections using **section heads**. All need to be checked. We have already mentioned page numbers, and these too require checking to ensure that they run in sequence.

Your volume may have the book title (or the chapter title, or the author's name, or a combination of these) printed at the top of each page. These are known as **pageheads** or **running heads** and need checking for both content and consistency (long titles may be shown in abbreviated form). Following the text comes the **endmatter**. A novel may contain no endmatter at all, or perhaps some publicity material for other books. (Non-fiction is a very different kettle of fish as we will see shortly.)

Finally there may be some **back-flap copy** (if the book is jacketed) and some **back copy** on the back cover. The title and author will probably also appear on the book's **spine**.

Works of non-fiction usually contain even more for you to worry about. The prelims may contain lists of **plates**, **figures**, **maps** and **tables**, notes on the **contributors** (in a multi-authored volume) and/or a list of **abbreviations**. The text may contain illustrations (with **captions**) and tables (with **titles**). These may be set upright on the page (**portrait**) or sideways (**landscape**). Pages set in landscape format should contain no running heads or page numbers and the foot of the illustration or table should always face to the right, irrespective of whether it appears on a recto or verso. The text may also contain **footnotes** (notes set at the foot of the page on which the **note indicator** appears) or **endnotes** (notes which appear either at the end of each chapter or in the endmatter). **References** to works cited in the text may also appear either at the end of each chapter or in the endmatter, and the book, or some chapters in it, may contain one or more **appendices**.

As well as the items mentioned above, the endmatter will usually contain an **index**, perhaps a **bibliography** (works listed in a reference section must be referred to in the text whereas works listed in a bibliography may or may not be mentioned; some works contain both a reference list and a bibliography) and sometimes a **glossary**. As you can see, there is much more to most books than meets the average reader's eye!

3 – Proofreading

The basic tools of the trade are a red pen, a blue pen, a pencil, an eraser and some correcting fluid. You also need somewhere to sit and a light source. Let's look at these in turn.

You will be making neat, precise corrections so a fine-nibbed pen is essential. An ordinary ballpoint pen is fine, although try not to use one that makes blobs on the page as this not only looks messy but, worse still, may make your corrections indecipherable.

You don't want to keep sharpening your pencil so buy a supply of plastic propelling 'clutch' pencils (the sort where pressing the end pushes up the lead). These are cheap enough to throw away, but if you're watching the pennies you can buy a pack of 0.7mm leads to use as refills.

Clutch pencils usually incorporate a pencil eraser, but you'll find that it soon gets used up so invest in a decent sized one that will last for ages.

Just as you will be making neat, precise corrections, so will you make neat, precise mistakes. The usual 'bottle and brush' method of applying correcting fluid may be rather too ham-fisted to delete tiny mistakes, and the extra you spend on a directable version (such as the Pentel Microcorrect) will be well worth while.

Now that you have the tools to work *with* you need something to work *on*. Any large flat surface will do. The kitchen table is fine – until teatime comes and you have to move all your carefully arranged papers. Better to invest in something you can call your own. There's no need to spend a fortune on a desk with half a dozen drawers (one drawer is useful, but not essential) – any old table will do as long as it's of a reasonable size (say 1.6m × 0.6m or 5ft × 2ft in old money). Try a car boot sale, second-hand shop or government surplus store – you'll be surprised what a few pounds can buy. Place your desk by a window if possible (facing north if you have a choice) and buy yourself a reading lamp. Use your lamp always – it helps to even out the light intensity. You will probably find that a 40 watt pearl bulb is strong enough.

One last point while we're on the subject of vision. If you don't wear spectacles already, consider taking an eye test to see if you would benefit from reading glasses. Proofreading puts quite a strain on the eyes and any slight defect in your eyesight will soon make itself apparent in the form of tiredness and headaches. Don't forget to claim the cost against tax!

Of course you will also need a telephone so that publishers can contact you with work, and a typewriter will come in handy for preparing **query sheets** (see pages 12 and 18) and to give your correspondence a more professional appearance. A fax machine and a computer may be nice to play with, but neither is essential.

You are now ready to begin proofreading. There are two types of error that a proofreader looks for. The first are mistakes that have been introduced into the proofs by the typesetter. It is easy to press a wrong key, overlook a comma or skip a line and even the most experienced keyboard operator will usually make a mistake or two. Such errors are marked in red and the cost of their correction is borne by the typesetter.

The second are errors that have been missed by the copy-editor and have been transferred by the typesetter from the typescript to the proofs. It is not a typesetter's job to spot mistakes in a typescript – they could, after all, be deliberate. In any event, the best typesetters input letter-by-letter and make no attempt even to read the words they are setting, let alone check them for sense and accuracy. These errors are marked in blue (some publishers prefer black or pencil), as are any revisions made by the author. Generally speaking, 'blue' corrections are paid for by the publisher, although correction costs in excess of 10 per cent of the original typesetting charge are usually passed on to the author. (In practice, '10 per cent' equates to a blue correction every couple of pages, *not* to resetting 10 per cent of the text. As you can see, corrections are expensive!) Because of the high cost of corrections, proofreaders need to exercise a degree of judgement when marking blues – in some cases it is better to ignore a missing hyphen or wrongly placed punctuation mark than to incur the cost of changing it. There is also the possibility that in making one correction the typesetter will introduce another mistake – this point is particularly important at the revise stage when corrections should definitely be kept to a minimum.

You will come across the terms **typo**, for typographical error, and **lit**, or **literal** error. Failure to indent a paragraph, for example, is a typo; a misspelling, for instance, is a literal. The distinction is not especially important – your job is simply to decide whether the correction should be made in red or blue. This is quite straightforward: use red if the typesetter has made a mistake, otherwise use blue.

It is also the proofreader's job to insert the page numbers on the contents page, check that running heads, captions, headings and pagination are correct and ensure that each page is set to the correct **depth** (i.e. has the correct number of lines of text).

You will also need to list any queries that you wish to raise: anything that doesn't seem quite right or that you are unsure whether to correct. Most publishers are happy for these to be marked in pencil on the proofs where they can be picked up by the editor when collating (but always mention any main points in a covering letter as well). You may, however, be required to list queries on a separate sheet – especially if they are questions that only the author can answer. Ask the publisher which they prefer.

You should query with the publisher anything that you are unsure of at proof stage, no matter how small (within reason). This is the last chance to correct an error before it is immortalized in print!

You may be asked to proofread either **against copy** or **blind** (sometimes known as **reading for sense**). When proofreading against copy you will receive both a set of proofs and the typescript. Your job is to compare one against the other. Proofreading is the exact opposite of speed-reading; you must read every letter of every word. Read a line from the proof, the same line on the typescript copy, a line from the proof, a line from the copy and so on. When proofreading blind you will receive a set of proofs only, and you must read them with equal care. Obviously, when reading blind you cannot allocate responsibility for errors, so all marks will be made in one colour – usually red unless the publisher has a preferred alternative. (*Note*: never use a green pen as this is the colour used by the typesetting company to mark any errors they may spot.)

When reading against copy it is easier to spot typesetter's errors whereas reading blind tends to elicit more lits and inconsistencies. Usually the professional freelance reads against copy and the author reads for sense, though some publishers send out proofs to two freelances as well as the author. Reading blind takes around one-third less time than reading against copy, but in either case be careful not to become engrossed in the book's contents – your job is to find the faults, not to read for pleasure!

4 – Correcting Proofs

Obviously it is impractical (and usually impracticable too) to write out proof corrections in longhand, so we use a series of **proofreading symbols** to instruct the typesetter what corrections to make. These symbols are divided into **textual marks** and **marginal marks** (see the Proofreading Symbols appendix for a list of these). The textual marks indicate where the change is to be made and the marginal marks indicate the correction required: for example, if you wished to change 'chose' to 'choose' you would put the textual mark for 'insert' between the 'o' and 's' of 'chose' and in the margin put the letter 'o' followed by the 'insert' symbol. To delete a word or letter, cross through it in the text and write the symbol for 'delete' in the margin (or 'delete and close up' if, for example, you were changing 'choose' to 'chose').

You will notice that the list gives both 'old style' and 'new style' marks. The 'old style' marks correspond to those given in British Standard 1219 and contain abbreviations for English words such as 's.o.' for 'spell out', 'cap' for capital letter' and so on. The 'new style' marks correspond to BS5261 part 2 and consist of symbols only – hence they are suitable for international use.

Unless the publisher has expressed a preference, I would suggest that you use the BS5261 marks, but you *must* use one or the other convention throughout, *never a mixture*.

When implementing your corrections, the typesetter will simply scan down the margins to find where the corrections are to be made. It is important, therefore, to ensure (a) that you *always* use a marginal mark (even if it is the same as the textual mark) and (b) that marginal marks appear *exactly* alongside the lines of text to which they relate. Time is money, and the more quickly a typesetter can find, identify and implement your corrections the lower will be the cost to the publisher. Keep this last point in mind as you work and don't be too clever with your symbols – if a single word requires two or three corrections it's probably better to cross it through and write the correct version in full in the margin. Every correction must be obvious and unambiguous.

Corrections to the left-hand half of a line are written in the left-hand margin and vice versa. Corrections should be written from left to right, so don't make your first left-hand marginal mark too close to the text in case you find additional mistakes in that half-line.

5 – Copy-editing

Contrary to popular belief, an editor's job is not to censor what is written, nor to 'cut it down to size'. A good copy-editor acts as an intermediary between author and reader, ensuring that the reader reads what the author intends them to. This is *not* always the same thing that the author has written!

The copy-editor needs to:

- mark up the typescript for the typesetter;
- check for grammatical, spelling and punctuation errors;
- impose consistency;
- ensure that the publisher's **house style** has been followed;
- read for sense;
- watch out for factual errors and libellous statements;
- make sure all illustrations and tables are present and correct;
- check notes and references;
- prepare a list of running heads;
- prepare caption copy for figures and illustrations;
- prepare lists of queries for author and publisher;
- prepare a word list and style sheet.

This is not a complete list (although it covers the essentials) – every book is different and you will find all aspects of the copy-editorial function covered in as much detail as you could ever need among the works listed in the 'Training' and 'Recommended Reference Books' sections. The above-listed points are common to most books though, and we shall consider them in turn.

Marking up the Typescript

Unlike proof correction, all editorial amendments are made on the typescript (**ts**) itself. Marginal marks are reserved for indicating the *style* of text to be used: for instance, a chapter title may be marked 'CT', a section heading 'A', a subsection head 'B', a quoted extract 'EXT' and so on. All such marks should be circled to indicate to the typesetter that they are not to be set. Similarly, any written instructions to the typesetter such as 'Please place Figure 1 near here' should also be circled. You must also, of course, take care *not* to encircle completely anything that is to be set.

In publishing terms, each page of the ts is known as a **folio** to distinguish it from a page of a book. Folios should be numbered consecutively throughout the ts – not by chapter as many authors do – and you may be required to number the ts if it has not already been done. (Some publishers prefer the prelims to be numbered A, B, C, etc. and the text 1, 2, 3.)

The ts should have been prepared using double-spaced lines, giving you plenty of room to write any amendments neatly above the original text. Never use correcting fluid to cover up original copy – the author should always be able to see exactly what has been done to the original. If a passage requires extensive modification or addition it may be better to type up the new copy on a separate sheet and instruct the typesetter to insert it at the appropriate point.

As with proofs, your instructions need to be crystal clear. Always read carefully and follow scrupulously any copy-editor's brief that may have been enclosed with the ts.

Grammar, Spelling and Punctuation

You don't need a degree in English to become a good copy-editor, but you will need to know the basic rules of grammar and punctuation. The training and reference books listed will provide all the guidance you require. Spelling isn't everybody's strong point and we all have a few words that trip us up. As long as you have a good dictionary and remember to look up *every* word that you are not 100 per cent sure of you will be fine. Remember that many American English words are spelt differently from their British English equivalents (and sometimes have different meanings altogether). Americans are also far more tolerant of 'bad' grammatical practices such as split infinitives ('to boldly go') and poor sentence construction. If you're a keen leisure reader of American fiction you may have picked up some bad habits!

Consistency

Many words and compounds may be spelt equally correctly in two or more ways: recognise/recognize; cooperate/co-operate; judgement/judgment (but always 'judgment' if it is being used in a legal context); focused/focussed; status quo/*status quo*; etc. Neither version is necessarily 'wrong' (but see 'house style' below); however, only *one* version should be used in any one book. Consistency should not usually be imposed on quoted matter – for instance an extract from an American work in a British text should retain its American spelling.

House Style

Many publishers ask their authors (and editors) to follow a house style – for example, to use -ize endings rather than -ise, lay out tables in a particular fashion, italicize certain words, always (or never) use full points following contractions and/or abbreviations and so on. You should be sent a copy of the publisher's house style guide with your first set of proofs. If you aren't then ask for one and ignore it at your peril!

Sense

Occasionally an author's brain works faster than his or her hands – make sure that each sentence is finished before the next one starts. Check also that Mr Smith doesn't become Mr Jones half way through the book, or that the dog that died in Chapter 2 doesn't turn up for its dinner in Chapter 27.

Factual Errors and Libel

You may be editing subjects ranging from abseiling to zoology, but you won't be expected to be an expert in all of them. Any errors of fact are ultimately the author's responsibility, but do watch out for obvious errors like England winning the World Cup in 1956 or dividing a cake into three halves. Instructions in 'how-to' books should be idiot-proof (unless obviously written for an expert readership) and should always carry appropriate warnings if potentially hazardous. Point out to the publisher anything that could conceivably land them in court or that may require permission to reproduce.

Illustrations and Tables

'Illustrations' is used here as a catch-all term for plates (photographs), drawings, graphs, figures, etc. Illustrations (and sometimes tables too) are often supplied separately. You will usually receive photocopies rather than the original **artwork**, so you can make any necessary corrections directly on to them. (Do check with the publisher if in any doubt – the last thing you want is to find that you have scrawled over someone's prized originals!) Check that each illustration is (a) referred to in the text (i.e. 'see Figure 2.1' etc.), (b) contains the information that the text says it does and (c) follows the style of the rest of the book in its labelling. Mark 'Fig. 2.1 near here please – allow $1/2$ page (or whatever)' in the margin of the relevant ts folio and mark 'Nr fo. 123' on the illustration itself. You may be asked to **flag** the relevant folios. This means attaching a small Post-It note, leaving the edge protruding so that the folios concerned can be found easily.

Tables need to be marked up to house style, checked for accuracy and, unless they are **embedded** in the ts (i.e. not supplied separately), you should mark 'Table 2.1 near here', and so on, as above.

Notes and References

Check that all note indicators are present and that the note indicated is relevant to the text at that point. The references are a list of printed or other sources that the author has made use of in preparing the book. All works mentioned in the text should be listed in the references and vice versa.

Running Heads

List these on a separate sheet, preferably typed. The usual format is 'book title on verso/chapter title on recto' for single-authored volumes; you may have to provide abbreviated versions of long chapter titles. You will find guidance on preparing running heads in the reference books listed on pages 26 and 28.

Caption Copy

Even if the **figure captions** are marked on the artwork you will still be required to produce a separate list for the typesetter to work from. All artwork is usually captioned, even if just the figure number ('Figure 2.1') is used (this is so that an unambiguous reference may be made in the text – e.g. 'see Figure 2.1', not 'see the figure two pages back'). **Table titles** are usually set at the same time as the text (as are the tables) and so require no separate listing.

Query Sheets

You will always have a few, often many, queries which only the author can answer, and these need to be listed. You need to include the following information for each: author's page number (e.g. Chapter 2, page 5); the ts folio number (from the continuous numbering sequence mentioned on page 15); the text line in which the query occurs and, of course, the query itself. Queries should be brief but polite (i.e. 'Something missing here?', not 'This doesn't make sense'). Make a separate list of anything the publisher should be aware of.

Word List and Style Sheet

Divide a sheet of A4 paper into squares labelled alphabetically and use it to record your decisions on spelling, hyphenation, capitalization, italicization, etc. as you work through the book. *Don't rely on your memory*. You should also compose a style sheet detailing what levels of heading you have used ('A', 'B', 'C', 'EXT', etc.) and where you have first used them, style for references and cross-references, elision of numbers (i.e. 122–123, 122–23 or 122–3; note that numbers between 10 and 19 are never elided, so use 112–16 even if the style is 122–3), and anything else you can think of. The word list and style sheet will help you, the typesetter and the proofreader to ensure that the book contains as few inconsistencies as possible. You do not have to worry about such things as whether headings will be in bold type or if extracts will be set in smaller type – just mark A, B, EXT, etc. and the designer will brief the typesetter on the typography required.

6 – Rewriting

It is not a copy-editor's job to change the wording or style of the ts simply because she or he prefers an alternative turn of phrase or form of punctuation. There are, however, occasions where an author is a poor writer! This apparent contradiction often occurs in leisure-interest or technical books where a person who is an expert and/or well-known in their field, but who is an inexperienced author, is asked to write a volume on their special subject. This can result in an informed but rather amateurish presentation which requires a good deal of rewriting before it is fit for publication. You do not have to be a professional writer to rewrite successfully, or an expert on the subject in question (although some knowledge is helpful of course). Good rewriting involves improvement of poor phraseology *without changing the author's intended meaning* in order to make the work both interesting and intelligible to the reader. These italicized words are most important. If the meaning is ambiguous as written, don't guess – query. Such authors are usually only too happy to accept your changes and will often thank you for improving their book. You may even get a credit in the acknowledgements!

Academic books do not suffer from this problem to such an extent. Most academic authors are quite practised in the art of writing for publication, having written at least an MA or PhD thesis and often also several journal articles. Having said this, take care when editing the work of an author whose first language is not English – such people often possess a far better grasp of their subject than they do of the English language.

Copy-editing fiction requires particular care and it is better to employ a very light hand. In most academic non-fiction books it is the argument that is paramount and the editing process is often geared to a large extent towards removing idiosyncrasies of style and presentation which would distract the reader from the author's line of reasoning. On the other hand, fiction (and associated read-for-pleasure material such as biography, 'true stories', etc.) is published and purchased for entertainment as much as enlightenment. An author's style is part and parcel of that and should not be tampered with. Query all changes except those involving punctuation and consistency (and even then be careful not to change a sentence construction that is intentionally unusual). Finally we come to dialogue: Spoken and written English are two very different animals. Few people speak 'correct' English and any author with a good ear will reflect this in written dialogue (or 'direct speech' as it is properly called). By all means query if dialogue seems out of character, but emendation of grammatically incorrect speech is rarely appropriate.

7 – Project Editing

Project editing (or project management) takes the copy-editing process a stage further and involves the use of a wider range of skills (which may be, though is not always, reflected in an hourly rate of £1 or more in excess of that for copy-editing).

A project editor will be expected to see a book through its various stages from raw typescript to passing for press. This may involve some or all of the following and perhaps more:

- In-depth discussion of general points of style, cost implications, etc. with your in-house contact.
- Copy-editing the ts.
- Checking illustrations.
- Chasing the author for any missing or late items.
- Resolving any queries with the author.
- Proofreading.
- Proof collation.
- Liaising with the designer.
- Checking the paste-up.
- Checking colour proofs.
- Preparing an index.
- Approving for publication.

As you can see, the project editor has a great deal more input to, and responsibility for, a book than the straightforward get-it/mark-it/send-it-back copy-editor. This can be rather unnerving, but ultimately very satisfying when 'your' book is published. You will need to have proved your competence as both proofreader and copy-editor before a publisher will consider you for a project, and of course it is both pointless and dishonest to offer your services for this type of work until you have gained the necessary skills and experience.

Not every publisher entrusts this type of work to freelances, and those that do naturally favour freelances living nearby who are available for the occasional in-house work that project editing necessitates.

8 – The Computer in Publishing

We have already mentioned the role of the computer in typesetting on page 7. There was a time when many people believed that the computer would make copy-editors redundant – just use a spell-check program, auto-check for consistency, and hey presto! – one perfect book.

Naturally it didn't take long to discover that a 'hunter with a bear behind' and a 'hunter with a bare behind' were both acceptable to the non-sense (nonsense?) reading computer so fear not, potential freelances, your jobs are safe (for the moment anyway!).

Of course, the computer has brought many benefits for authors and publishers alike. The advent of desktop publishing means that print runs of as few as 50 can be economically viable (more work for us) and that errors are now much easier both to avoid and to correct.

Many typescripts are prepared on disk and many copy-editors do carry out on-screen editing. Computer skills and the possession of suitable hardware are becoming increasingly desirable qualities in a copy-editor, much less so for a proofreader, but they are in no way essential for success as a freelance, as I know from experience.

When editing a **hard-copy** (i.e. paper) ts which has been prepared on disk you may be asked to make marginal as well as textual marks so that the typesetter can incorporate your changes in much the same way as they would a proofreader's corrections. (Since the text is already 'set' on the disk there is no need for the typesetter to read every word – just the ones which need to be changed.)

One very useful spin-off from on-disk ts production is the ability to input **global corrections**. For instance, if a word has been frequently misspelt, or spelt in a variety of ways, it can be made consistent throughout with one global correction. Commands indenting paragraphs, inserting spaces either side of a dash and so on can also be entered globally. Be careful how you use such corrections though – global -ise or -ize endings could make someone a prise idiot or have them prizing open a manhole cover!

9 – Other Freelance Opportunities

By far the majority of freelances in publishing are copy-editors and/or proofreaders, but there are some other avenues that you may wish to explore.

Although the computer age has made it far easier for authors to compile indexes for their own books, many publishers still prefer to utilize the services of a professional **indexer** for this task. A specialist indexer often has better judgement with respect to what should and should not be indexed, the correct presentation of index entries, suitable cross-references and so on. Indexing is a skilled and complex process, and as a copy-editor you would be unwise to attempt the compilation of any but the simplest index without training.

Book **design** is another area colonized by freelances. Virtually all publishers have at least one designer on their staff, but much design work is also contracted out. The design task includes making decisions on the size and style of typeface to be used for text, headings, captions and displayed matter (the designer may mark these instructions for the typesetter on the edited ts following the copy-editor's marginal codes), cutting and pasting-up the galley proofs on to the layout, deciding positions of illustrations and photographs and selecting which photographs to use.

Fluency in a second language may enable you to get work as a freelance **translator**, although your language skills must be perfect and you will require specialist knowledge in *both* languages for any remotely technical matter.

If you are of an artistic nature you may consider offering your services as an **illustrator** in addition to your proofreading and editorial skills, so giving yourself two bites of the freelance cherry.

Along similar lines, many books require the commissioning of freelance **photography** to illustrate the contents. Many standard or general pictures may be obtained from a picture library (another potential market for your pictures) and the author may also supply transparencies to accompany the ts. None the less, there is still some potential for the keen and competent amateur photographer to make money from their hobby.

10 – Societies and Associations

Anyone wishing to pursue a career as a freelance proofreader or copy-editor is well advised to join the **Society of Freelance Editors and Proofreaders**. The aim of the SFEP is to encourage high standards of editing and proofreading and to promote training and qualification. Your membership subscription entitles you to receive a copy of the SFEP's monthly newsletter which contains much useful information and articles of interest to the publishing freelance. Members are able to attend SFEP-organized training courses (see page 26) at reduced rates and also have the opportunity to buy a wide range of reference books at discounted prices from the Society's booklist. You may also purchase an entry in the SFEP Directory, over 1,500 of which are circulated throughout the publishing industry each year.

Perhaps just as important is the fact that you are able to include the words 'Member of the Society of Freelance Editors and Proofreaders' on your stationery (although you may *not* use the SFEP logo). The SFEP does not guarantee the work of its members (although it is introducing an accreditation scheme whereby members of proven high calibre will be able to describe themselves as 'Accredited' or 'Registered Member of the SFEP'), but the mere fact that you have joined should indicate to a publisher that you are at least taking your freelance career seriously.

The SFEP's address will be found on page 57. You may be asked for a deposit in return for their information pack, to be offset against your first year's membership fee. You might also be informed that freelance work is sporadic and difficult to obtain. These measures are to weed out the merely curious from the committed. (For my personal opinion, see page 38.)

The **Society of Indexers** will provide advice on training as a specialist indexer and will also recommend competent members to enquiring authors and publishers. They too publish an annual directory 'Indexers Available' as well as a journal *The Indexer* (free to members).

The **Translators' Association**, part of the Society of Authors, gives advice on all aspects of translating into English including legal advice, marketing and rates.

Illustrators may find the **Association of Illustrators** of interest, whose aim is to improve relationships among illustrators, agents and clients. The **Master Photographers' Association** does much the same for photographers.

There are many other societies and associations connected with the publishing world, full details of which will be found in the *Writers' and Artists' Yearbook*.

11 – What Makes a Good Freelance?

There are two areas for us to consider here. The first is your personal circumstances; the second is the type of person you are.

One requisite for any proofreader or copy-editor is peace and quiet. This is a job that requires 100 per cent concentration and you can hardly expect to give of your best if you are likely to suffer continual interruption. Ideally you need to find a corner, or better a spare room, where you can set up an office for yourself. Extraneous noise need not be too problematic – foam ear-plugs make very effective barriers against all but the loudest TV sets, hi-fis and children – but you must make it clear to family and friends that when you are working you need to be treated as though you were invisible.

People tend to confuse working on a book with reading for pleasure, and your work will suffer if you are up and down every few minutes to feed the cat, change a plug, or do any of the thousand and one other little tasks that you might be doing were you a person of leisure. Working from home means just that – *working* from home – and you should be no more accessible than if you were in an office or factory several miles away.

Having said that, of course, working from home does have obvious advantages, but make sure it's *you* who decides when to make a cup of tea or weed the garden when you feel like a break.

One great advantage of freelancing is the ultimate flexibility it offers when it comes to choosing your hours of work. You can freelance full time if you wish, or work just a couple of days a week or a few hours a day. You can work mornings, evenings or nights if you want to and have a day off whenever you like (finances and publishers' deadlines permitting) – it makes no difference to your employer as long as the work is done well and returned on time.

The majority, if not all, of your work will arrive and be returned by post (or carrier), so effectively where you live is unimportant. (Most of the publishers I work for are based at least 200 miles from my home in Devon.) It also means that you can move to any part of the country that takes your fancy, as long as it has daily postal deliveries, without losing or changing your job. Perhaps one day the same may be said of anywhere in the European Union.

The other side of the 'freedom' coin bring us to the first of those personal qualities you must possess – self-discipline. There is no hiding from the fact that you and you alone are responsible for organizing your time to ensure that your work is carried out properly and promptly. There is no one to tell you off for bad timekeeping or laziness – if you spend the afternoon watching TV or sunbathing you have no one to blame but yourself.

One thing you *don't* have to be is a linguistic genius. Obviously you must be able to spell competently or you will fail to spot literal errors, and a flair for

English is desirable, but the rules of grammar and punctuation can be learnt just like any other skill. Qualifications such as a degree are useful if you hope to specialize in a particular technical or scientific subject, but most people have a good knowledge of one or two special interests or hobbies about which they can offer their expertise. It also helps if you are one of those annoying people who always seem to win Trivial Pursuit!

As we mentioned earlier, powers of concentration are important and something you must possess in abundance. You can take a five-minute break every hour to give your eyes a rest, but for the other 55 minutes you will need to keep all your wits about you. As with most skills, your ability to concentrate will improve with practice.

A methodical mind is also helpful. As you will discover, much of the job comprises making lists and ensuring consistency of presentation and style. The more methodical you are, the fewer inconsistencies will appear in your work and the more work you will get.

Finally, you require an eye for detail to spot those 'little' errors like a missing full stop or quotation mark which are so easy to overlook at the proof stage but which stand out like sore thumbs once the book is in print! Once again, you will improve with practice and training.

12 – Training

As in any field, there are certain skills you must acquire in order to become competent in your new career. Fortunately, a variety of training resources are available. To learn the basics of proofreading is not difficult, and as long as you have a good basic knowledge of English and have mastered the proofreading symbols on page 53 there is no reason why you should not start earning straight away.

If you wish to progress beyond the basics, however, you will need to put in a little more effort. You can do this either at home or at an educational institution. Which you choose will depend on your other commitments, your geographical location and the depth of your pockets.

You may see a number of correspondence or home-study courses advertised for freelancing costing up to £100 or more. These are fine as far as they go; consider them by all means, but bear in mind that these are unlikely to lead to a recognized qualification in publishing (although of course publishers may be impressed by the fact that you are showing willing).

However, if you are good at self-tuition you can do no better than to purchase a copy of Nicola Harris's *Basic Editing: A Practical Course* (published by Book House Training Centre/UNESCO). *Basic Editing* comes in two volumes: *The Text* and *The Exercises*. The course is divided into 32 units which between them cover all the elements of competence identified in Units 1 to 4 of the National Vocational Qualification requirements for a copy-editor (see below for more on NVQs). This of course includes proofreading as well as copy-editing. The combined cost of the two volumes is around £30 (cheaper through the SFEP). Highly recommended.

The drawback of learning at home of course is that there is no one handy of whom you can ask questions if you get stuck (though joining your regional SFEP group may help). The SFEP runs a number of training workshops in London, York and Edinburgh (more venues are planned), each usually lasting one day. The courses include Introduction to Proofreading, Proofreading Problems, Introduction to Copy-editing, Efficient Copy-editing, References, Introduction to Illustrations, Marking up Manuscripts for Interfacing, Personal Effectiveness, Going Freelance and Staying There, Running a One-Person Business and Brush up your Grammar. These are open to all with costs ranging from around £40–50 for SFEP members and £75–85 for non-members.

The Book House Training Centre in London (address on page 57) also offers regular training sessions and a distance-learning course based on *Basic Editing*. *On Course*, the BHTC newsletter, is published three times a year and distributed free of charge. Contact the Editor if you wish to be put on their mailing list.

The Paul Hamlyn Foundation is a registered charity committed to working to advance the role of training and skills development in the publishing industry. In 1996, £15,000 was made available by the Foundation to support freelances wishing to develop their skills through training and they have also in the past offered help towards the cost of NVQs in publishing. Grants are allocated at the start of the financial year, so apply early. The Foundation's address is Sussex House, 12 Upper Mall, London W6 9TA; Tel.: 0181-741 2812. Training organizations recognized by the Foundation include the following:

- *Book House Training Centre* (address on page 57).
- *Chapterhouse Publishing*, 2 Southernhay West, Exeter EX1 1JG. *Tel.:* 01392 498008.
- *London College of Printing & Distributive Trades*, Elephant and Castle, London SE1 6SB. *Tel.:* 0171-735 8484.
- *London School of Publishing*, David Game House, 69 Notting Hill Gate, London W11 3JS. *Tel.:* 0171-221 3399.
- *Mayflower Computing Consultants*, Ro Dew, West Looe Hill, Looe, Cornwall PL13 2HH. *Tel.:* 01503 263688.
- *Oxford Brookes University*, Gipsy Lane, Headington, Oxford OX3 0BP. *Tel.:* 01865 741111.
- *The Oxford Publicity Partnership*, 12 Hid's Copse Road, Cumnor Hill, Oxford OX2 9JJ. *Tel.:* 01865 865466.
- *Password Training*, 23 New Mount Street, Manchester M4 4DE. *Tel.:* 0161-953 4009.
- *PMA Training*, The Old Anchor, Church Street, Hemingford Grey, Cambs PE18 9DF. *Tel.:* 01480 300653.
- *The Scottish Book Centre* (address on page 57).
- *The Society of Freelance Editors and Proofreaders* (address on page 57).
- *The Society of Indexers* (address on page 57).
- *Training Matters*, 15 Pitts Road, Headington Quarry, Oxford OX3 8BA. *Tel.:* 01865 66964.
- *West Herts College*, Hempstead Road, Watford, Herts. WD1 3EZ. *Tel.:* 01923 257654.

There are doubtless many other educational establishments throughout the country offering suitable courses. Try your local centres and compare course coverage with the *Basic Editing* contents to gauge how comprehensive they are.

National Vocational Qualifications (NVQs)

NVQs are now available in most work-related areas and publishing is no exception. You do not need an NVQ to become a successful freelance at the moment, but it will certainly do your prospects no harm to have one. NVQs are 'on-the-job' qualifications involving the proving of your mastery of various designated areas of competence, and may thus only be embarked upon once your freelance career is well established. Full details can then be obtained from the Publishing Qualifications Board, 344–354 Gray's Inn Road, London WC1X 8BP; Tel.: 0171-278 4411.

13 – Recommended Reference Books

To embark on a career as a freelance proofreader you must at least possess a good dictionary. The two most popular are the *Concise Oxford* and *Chambers*, the latter having rather more entries and being somewhat less prescriptive than the former. Expect to pay £13 to £20. (Note: All prices given in this section are approximate and should be used for guidance only. You will probably save a few pounds on certain volumes if you buy through the SFEP.)

The Oxford Writers' Dictionary (£7) is a useful companion volume which includes many proper names, abbreviations, italicizations and hyphenations. *The Oxford Spelling Dictionary* (£5), as well as being a handy reference for a word's spelling (as opposed to its meaning), gives recommended **word breaks** (i.e. where to put the hyphen if a word has to be broken at the end of a line), which can save you the embarrassment of replacing a bad break in a proof with an equally poor one of your own!

Hart's Rules for Compositors and Readers (39th edition), also published by Oxford University Press (£9), has helpful sections on hyphenated and italicized words, punctuation, etc., but the *Oxford Writers' Dictionary* is probably the better choice if you cannot afford both. A volume combining the two titles is planned.

When you expand your repertoire to include copy-editing you will also need to expand your reference library. The copy-editor's 'Bible' is *Copy-Editing* by Judith Butcher (3rd edition), published by Cambridge University Press (£19). This is one book that no copy-editor can afford to be without and it contains the answers to most of the queries you will ever have regarding the copy-editing process.

Fowler's Modern English Usage (OUP – £7) is an informative and often witty volume explaining not just how words should be used but also why. *Fowler's* is idiosyncratic in places, to say the least, and his prescriptions in some cases are best taken with a pinch of salt, but it is a mine of information for all that, especially if like me you don't have the benefit of a classical education. Along much the same lines is Eric Partridge's *Usage and Abusage*, a new edition of which was published by Penguin in 1995. Either Fowler or Partridge will serve you well, but you won't need both.

A thesaurus is always useful, especially when dealing with authors whose vocabulary is rather limited. *Roget's Thesaurus* is the best known and is offered by several publishers at a variety of prices. *Chambers Thesaurus* is well regarded, if a little expensive at around £13.

If you are editing books for the American market, the *Chicago Manual of Style* (14th edition) is the standard work (University of Chicago Press – £35). This contains in-depth coverage of most aspects of US style and book production and is useful for UK-based editors who are experienced enough to appreciate the many subtle differences between British and American style (as you soon will be). You will also need an American dictionary. *Webster's* is a good choice, including as it does recommended word division, and Biographical and Geographical lists at the back.

It will pay you to buy new copies of any of the aforementioned works since writing style is as subject to the vagaries of fashion as anything else, and of course new words are constantly being added to the language to cater for popular trends. As an inexperienced freelance, to learn using outdated information could prove disastrous.

You can, however, make many useful additions to your reference library by purchasing other books second hand, often for only a few pence. *Pears Cyclopaedia* is a handy little volume, published annually, copies of which can often be picked up for under a pound at car boot sales or charity shops. This contains a list of important events from the year dot, prominent people, a gazetteer, conversion tables, a political compendium, etc., plus each year a variety of special subject sections. Any book with the title *A Dictionary of . . .* should be snapped up whether the subject is one of your specialisms or not. You will be surprised at how often the right book on your shelf will save you hours of searching elsewhere.

It will also pay you to make your own list of 'difficult' names that appear in the news – but make sure that the source you're using is accurate: newspapers are infamous for literals!

A collection of foreign-language to English dictionaries will prove their worth – the little Collins Gem or Harrap's Mini range will be adequate for most of the odd words you are likely to encounter in general work.

Atlases, biographical dictionaries, almanacs – all is grist to the mill. Keep your eyes open in junk shops and at jumble sales and if it's cheap, buy it.

You will find useful works on indexing, design and other areas of publishing listed in the Bibliography on page 91 and in the SFEP booklist.

14 – Getting Started

Freelance proofreading and copy-editing is one of the few professional occupations that require no qualifications to enter. This is a two-edged sword in that while publishers cannot hold a lack of formal qualifications against you, neither have they any yardstick by which to judge the abilities of an untried freelance.

Publishers are in business to sell books – a poor review of a badly produced book may not only adversely affect sales of the volume concerned but also, and much more seriously, damage the publisher's reputation. Before entrusting work to a freelance, therefore, a publisher must be confident that the work will be carried out to a high standard.

This creates a catch-22 situation whereby it is difficult to obtain work without experience and impossible to obtain experience without work! Having defined the problem, let's consider its solution – and make no mistake, the problem *is* soluble.

Even if you know *Basic Editing* and *Copy Editing* forwards, backwards and inside out you are most unlikely to be entrusted with any copy-editing project until you have proved your worth as a proofreader. Some publishers (though by no means all) send out proofreading and/or copy-editorial test pages to enquirers; others simply send you your first job – but we're jumping the gun a little now.

How are you to obtain that elusive first set of proofs? First, find your publisher. Not every publisher uses freelances, but we have made this stage easier for you by providing on page 39 a list of 101 organizations all of whom have contracted out freelance proofreading and/or copy-editorial work in the recent past. You will find many more in one of the several trade directories available at your local reference library.

Cold Calling

Your initial contact should be by telephone. 'Cold calling' (as such unsolicited approaches are known) can be a daunting prospect, especially if you are unused to using the telephone, but don't worry – once you've made a few calls you'll soon get the hang of it. You will find it much easier if you know in advance what you are going to say, what questions you are likely to be asked and what your replies will be.

Before making your call, have a sheet of paper handy, headed with the name and telephone number of the publisher you are calling and the types of books they publish. This is your 'information sheet'.

The telephone will be answered by the switchboard operator and this person will provide you with some vital information. Your first question should be along the lines of: 'Good afternoon, I wonder if you could tell me who is the person responsible at (name of company) for the placement of your freelance proofreading and copy-editorial work?' Write down the answer on your information sheet. Find out as much as you can about your contact: first name (or at least initial), position in the company, Mr/Mrs/Miss/Ms. Be polite and friendly and try to sound confident – after all, you're professional, good at your job, and a working relationship will benefit them as well as you. If the switchboard operator doesn't know who deals with freelance work, ask to be put through to Editorial and repeat your questions to whoever answers.

If you're feeling bold, another way to approach matters is to ask for either the managing director or the editorial director by name (you will find directors' names listed in the *Writers' and Artists' Yearbook*). You're unlikely to get through, but you can elicit the above information from the director's secretary (or the director in person if you are lucky). This has the advantage that, when you do get through to the right person in the Editorial department, you can say 'Pat Jones, your managing director, suggested that I call you . . .'

When you have all the information you need, ask to be put through to your contact. Publishing offices are quite friendly places and tend to operate on a first-name basis so, when the extension is picked up, say: 'Good afternoon, could I speak to Chris Smith please?' (If Chris Smith is out or busy don't leave a message – call back later.)

You should now be talking to the right person. They are busy, so don't waste their time. Be businesslike, confident and get straight to the point: 'Hello, my name's X. I'm a freelance proofreader and I'd like to enquire into the possibility of undertaking some assignments for (name of company).'

Don't be disappointed if the response is less than encouraging – yours will probably not be the first call received that week, or even that day. If a publisher tells you their pool of freelances is full they are merely being honest – not just trying to get rid of you. Nevertheless, a good editor will always be on the lookout for a good new freelance so don't just apologize for wasting their time and hang up. Say that you appreciate their position but that you really are keen to work for their company and ask if you could at least be sent a proofreading test so that your name can be added to their standby list should an unexpected influx of work arrive.

If this produces a negative response then at least obtain permission to forward your CV for future reference (see below). Ask if they would mind you ringing again in a few weeks' time to see if the situation has changed. Ask if they know of anyone else you could approach, either within their own organization or elsewhere – sometimes placement of work is the responsibility of more than one person and the left hand doesn't always know what the right one is looking for. Use your information sheet to summarize the call and jot down any lessons learnt that you can profitably use in subsequent calls to this or any other publisher.

Obviously we cannot predict every question that you will be asked, nor script your responses, but there are two that crop up frequently and which each have both correct and inappropriate responses.

For the newcomer, the most difficult question is 'What experience do you have?' The answer you must never give is 'None'. Do not tell lies, but emphasize what you *have* done rather than what you haven't. Admit that you have only recently turned freelance by all means, but balance this with any training you have undertaken – even if this is no more than self-tuition from *Basic Editing* you are at least demonstrating that you are taking the matter seriously. Emphasize any 'other' work you may have done (see page 37). If you have been accepted into another publisher's freelance pool then say so, even if you haven't yet carried out an assignment for them.

The second popular question is 'What do you specialize in?' The wrong answer here is 'Anything'. Publishers tend to dislike generalists, regarding them as knowing a little about everything and not a great deal about anything. (This theory is, in fact, quite contrary to practice, for you will find that once you are on a publisher's list they are indeed likely to throw 'anything' at you!) Before starting your telephone campaign, consider in which areas you could describe yourself as something of an expert. Have you a degree? A-levels? Hobbies? Interests? Work experience? Nearly everyone knows a lot about *something*. Study the listing starting on page 39 and contact companies who publish in your specialist fields. There is no point in impressing a contact with your knowledge of nuclear physics if all they publish is children's fiction. If possible, ask if there are any areas in which the publisher is short of freelance expertise and then tell them that's one of your specialist subjects (but only if it *is* – any attempt at deception will harm both the publisher and your prospects).

You may also be asked how much you charge. See page 35 for more information on rates.

Make your calls either between 10 a.m. and noon or 2 p.m. and 4 p.m. Avoid Monday mornings and Friday afternoons. Remember that you are selling yourself – don't be pushy but don't be timid either. You are in business to provide a valuable service. You are an efficient, reliable freelance. Act like one!

Your skill at cold calling will grow as you make more calls, so if there are any publishers that you really want to impress, don't contact them until you are sure that you can handle yourself with confidence.

Submitting your CV

Having successfully overcome the first hurdle, your next step is to follow up with a brief letter and CV. This serves as a reminder of your conversation, provides further information about you and gives the publisher something to put in their records. Your letter should preferably be handwritten – neatly of course: you are proposing to write all over their typescripts and proofs so it doesn't hurt to show your prospect that you possess a tidy hand. If your handwriting is dreadful then perhaps you should type your letter, but you'll need to work on your penmanship or you'll place yourself at a disadvantage. Address your letter to your contact, mention your telephone conversation and any salient points arising from it. Say that you are enclosing your CV and that you will contact them again shortly to ensure that it has been received safely. Personalize your letter by mentioning the name of the company – whatever you do, don't type a standard letter and photocopy it to save time. Treat each publisher as though they are your only hope of obtaining work. Make your letter businesslike, brief (no more than one A4 page long) and to the point.

Your CV should also be no more than one page long and typewritten. (You can mass-produce this if you wish, although again a personalized version would be better.) You should include your name, address, telephone number, date of birth, educational qualifications, any relevant training, freelance experience (if any), work experience (don't list all your jobs with dates, but do mention anything that supports your claim to any specialist knowledge), special interests (list here the areas of expertise identified earlier), equipment available (computer system, fax, photocopier) and other information ('available for occasional in-house work', 'can type at 120 wpm', etc.).

You will go a long way towards creating a professional impression by submitting your letter and CV on professionally printed stationery. This not only creates an aura of established professionalism, but also demonstrates that your application is serious rather than speculative. You will need letterheads and compliment slips at the very least. Letterheads can double as invoices or you may elect to have your invoices printed separately. Business cards are not essential unless you plan to visit your prospects in person.

It goes without saying that both your letter and CV must contain no errors of grammar or spelling. Presentation is of the utmost importance; publishers receive many letters like yours and you must ensure that yours stands out from the rest to have any chance of success.

Of course you will not be successful with every publisher you approach. Indeed, you might send out 50 or 100 letters and receive only one or two proofreading tests for your trouble. Don't despair – it's the same for all of us; and fortunately there are an awful lot of publishers to approach. With perseverance you *will* succeed if you really want to.

Consider for a moment your ultimate goal. What does 'success' mean? How many 'right notes' do you need to strike? Let's assume you want to work full time – say 30 hours of actual work a week (most people's '8-hour day' is really a 6-hour day with lunch and coffee breaks). A book will take, on average, 18 to 24 hours to complete – say 3 days' work – and a publisher will send an established freelance, on average, one book a month or around 40 days' work a year. If you work a 48-week (240-day) year you therefore need regular work from just six of Britain's 1,500 or so publishers to keep you fully occupied. Put this way, the problem seems far less daunting, doesn't it?

Test Pieces

You've made your cold calls, sent out your first 50 CVs, made your follow-up phone calls and received your first proofreading test. This may look simple but don't be deceived by appearances – it will contain a range of errors designed to test your abilities to the full. If the publisher has enclosed a style guide, ensure that you follow it to the letter. Mark the piece in pencil first and go over in red ink afterwards (don't worry about trying to decide which corrections are 'reds' and which are 'blues' unless your test piece is to be read against copy). Pay particular attention to consistency of spelling (-ise and -ize endings; judgment/judgement; cooperate/co-operate), presentation (thirty children sitting on 30 chairs), punctuation (red, white, and blue/red, white and blue; ''Yes,'' said John/'No,' said Jane) and content (a red jumper changing to a blue cardigan etc.). There will also be grammatical errors for you to spot: incorrect usage of less/fewer, better/best, that/which, etc. are popular. Consult Fowler or Partridge (see page 28) if you are unsure and check the spelling of any word of which you are not 100 per cent certain.

Part of a proofreader's skill lies in judging which errors are not cost-effective to correct. It may be better to let the odd misplaced comma or missing hyphen stand rather than incurring correction costs, and the test may be designed to examine your ability in this respect (remember, the publisher pays for blue corrections only). The answer here is to mark any such borderline corrections in pencil and explain to the publisher what you have done and why. (In a 'real-life' situation, the person at the publisher's collating the proofs would decide whether to incorporate your pencilled marks or not, simply erasing them in the latter case.)

Any inconsistencies that cannot be resolved with certainty should be marked with a marginal pencilled question mark and listed on a separate sheet headed 'Author Queries'. Queries should give the page number, line number and a *succinct* query, for example:

p. 1, line 4 – Fred Smith here but John Smith on p. 2, line 6.

p. 4, 3 lines up – Something missing between (. . .) and (. . .)?

Your list of queries should preferably be typed and double-spaced. Finally, re-read the test piece for sense.

Copy-editing test pieces must be treated with similar care, but of course you will be expected to correct all errors, no matter how trivial (corrections cost the publisher nothing at this stage), and possibly do a little rewriting (list any rewrites as Author Queries, e.g.: 'Change ''ABC'' to ''XYZ''?'). Your list of Author Queries will probably be longer for a copy-editing test than for a proofreading test. Don't forget to mark up the piece for the typesetter with levels of heading, marginal marks for extracts, displayed matter and so on. Run through the copy-editing checklist on page 15 and make sure you've covered everything.

You may be asked to state how long you spent on the test piece. Publishers normally expect a rate of around 8–12 pages per hour for text books, 12–15 for novels, when proofreading against copy (about 50 per cent more if reading blind) and a similar number of typescript folios per hour when copy-editing. (See page 35 for more on speed of work and rates of pay.) You will probably spend much longer than this on your test pieces – it may be wiser to advise your publisher what rate of work they can expect from you rather than being too specific about your test-piece time.

Return your test with a covering letter thanking the publisher, explaining what you have done, answering any questions that may have accompanied the test, and requesting the publisher's comments on your performance. This last point is vital: you can learn from any adverse comments but, much more important, a complimentary letter stating that you have completed the test well and will be considered for future projects can be photocopied and sent out to prospective clients as evidence of your competence.

Ring after a day or two to ensure that your test has been received safely. Ask if any work is available at the moment. If not, ask if you can ring again in a couple of weeks' time. Do so, saying: 'You asked me to call . . .' Repeat this process – your persistence will pay off eventually.

Maintain your telephone campaign, contacting new publishers and following up on those you have already contacted. Write second letters enclosing any evidence of competence you have collected. Follow the advice given in this guide, keep at it, and eventually you will receive that cherished phone call asking if you are free to work on a set of proofs. Suddenly it's all worth while!

Your First Assignment

This first set of proofs are the most important you will ever receive – make a mess of them and you will never hear from that publisher again. Treat your first project as an extended test piece. Time yourself by all means, but expect to invoice only about two-thirds of the time you actually spend after checking and double-checking everything. There will be plenty of time for you to earn a better rate once you've established your efficiency and reliability.

You will normally be given around two weeks to complete the work. Ensure that you meet your deadline, preferably with a few days to spare. If you are unsure of anything (e.g. house style), or come across a major problem, don't guess – ring for advice. Far better to spend a few minutes now sorting out the ground rules than to waste several hours marking up incorrectly. Return your work by first-class letter post (unless instructed otherwise) with a thankyou letter, detailing anything of which the publisher should be aware, and again ask for comments to increase your 'evidence of competence' file. (Publishers may be too busy to write a detailed reply, but even an acknowledgement is useful.) Phone a day or two later to ensure that your work has arrived safely and to ask if there is any more in the offing. (Don't expect an instant appraisal of your work at this time – the proofs will probably not have been collated yet.) Again, maintain regular telephone contact. This is not the time to worry about your telephone bill – it won't be long before the publishers are ringing you.

Rates of Work, Rates of Pay

The rates of pay offered by publishers vary enormously. As a rough guide you may be offered £7 to £9 per hour for proofreading and £8 to £10.50 per hour for copy-editing. Publishers also differ in their estimation of what constitutes an hour's work. Some are quite helpful in offering guidance – their brief to you may contain something along the lines of: 'I would expect this job to take between 30 and 35 hours' and you will usually find that this will correspond to your working at a rate of something like 10 to 15 pages per hour as discussed above. Occasionally, a book is being produced on a tight budget and you may be asked to spend, say, 'not more than 25 hours' on a 400-page manuscript. In such cases the publisher will appreciate that you are being asked to work quickly and will therefore not be surprised if you do a slightly less-thorough job than usual (for instance, you would not be expected to carry out any rewriting if copy-editing or to correct minor errors of punctuation or small inconsistencies of style if proofreading; you would, however, still be expected to spot all the lits and typos). Another method is for the publisher to advise you that 'The budget for this job is £300'. Any budget figure given is a maximum (ask if it includes your expenses such as telephone and postage); try to come in a little under it if you can. Still other publishers will just tell you their hourly rate and trust you to tell them how long the work has taken.

You will sometimes, though by no means always, find that publishers who offer lower rates are a little more generous with their time allowances while the better payers expect a faster performance for their money. As a novice you would be well advised to take whatever work you can get – experience is more important than money at this stage – but as you progress you will be able to become more selective.

Time your work at first. Don't be surprised if you average as few as seven pages an hour to begin with; you will soon increase your speed without sacrificing accuracy and you should be able to double this figure without too much difficulty. If you are working an eight-hour day you should aim to earn around £300 for a five-day week. We are not reading machines, and publishers realize that we need to rest our eyes for five minutes an hour, take lunch breaks and so on. Their expected rates of work reflect this – if you read 80 pages in six hours of *actual* work over an eight-hour day and the publisher is expecting 10 pages an hour, then don't be afraid to book eight hours rather than six. At a rate of £7.50 per hour, this would earn you £60, an *actual* hourly rate of £10.

You may feel that you can work even more quickly and so increase your earnings. This is not recommended; not only will you be betraying your client's trust in you to do a conscientious and thorough job, but rushing your work is the surest way to overlook errors. Your publisher is unlikely to give you a second chance; there are too many others only too willing to step into your shoes should you do a poor job. You have worked hard to establish your position – don't jeopardize it for the sake of a few pounds.

Occasionally you will be asked what your charges are. Try to be flexible and put the ball back in their court if you can by saying something such as: 'About £8 to £10 an hour depending on the task and the nature of the material; what do you usually pay?'

Your hourly rate is net of expenses (and VAT if you are registered), so add the costs of postage, telephone calls, etc. to your invoice. Your invoice may either be enclosed with the manuscript (you can usually calculate the cost of postage fairly accurately using the kitchen scales) or sent under separate cover.

You should ask the publisher what their payment arrangements are when they offer you your first job. Most pay within 30 days, some take six weeks, some are quicker. Telephone your contact with a friendly reminder if payment is late. Be wary of taking on more work from a publisher from whom payment is overdue (few are dishonest, but inevitably some may be in financial difficulties). Keep copies of all your invoices and receipts for all your expenses – the tax (wo)man will want to see them one day.

Keep an index card for each publisher containing name, address, telephone number, hourly rates, payment arrangements, contact name(s), any special requirements. On the back, list the jobs you do for them: date, title, extent (i.e. number of pages), hours booked, invoice amount and invoice number.

A few publishers pay 'peanuts' – under £6 an hour. Don't take work from them unless you're really desperate for experience, and then drop them as soon as you find someone more reasonable. If they won't pay a proper rate for a professional service they deserve no better treatment.

Other Approaches

We have concentrated so far on finding work with British publishing companies. Indeed this is your goal, but there are other avenues you might profitably explore along the way to provide you with both extra income and some vital experience to bolster a possibly flimsy CV.

Remember that virtually every word you read should have been proofread by somebody (although the numerous 'howlers' you can spot daily testifies that this is not always the case).

An obvious candidate for your emerging talent is the local printing fraternity. Many printers are poor proofreaders and even worse editors. Even if they follow their clients' copy to the letter, any mistakes will be classed as 'printer's errors' and so damage their reputation. Why not offer your services to them? Perhaps you could also convince them of the merits of offering a copy-editorial service to their clients who may wish to produce anything from a sales letter to a school magazine. Typesetting companies may also require your services, perhaps to supplement their in-house staff during busy periods.

Most businesses produce lots of literature: brochures, staff magazines, labels, packaging. Usually there is no one on the staff with the specialist skills necessary to edit or proofread such material and they may be oblivious of the fact that poorly produced literature will damage their prestige – unless you point it out to them. Try contacting the marketing managers of some local companies.

Contact the editorial offices of your local papers (the free sheets too) and any magazines produced in your area (consult *Willings Press Guide* at your local reference library for a full list of magazine/newspaper titles and their publishers). Advertising agencies and television programme makers are other potential sources of work. Try also your local council offices, schools, colleges, university, union offices, clubs, societies. Who proofreads the programmes for your town's football club or theatre? Your parish magazine? The list seems endless.

There are many agencies acting as middlemen between freelances and publishers. (You will find these listed under 'Services to Publishers' in the trade directories at the library – try *Kelly's*, and ask the librarian to recommend any others available.) It will do you no harm to be registered with them and you may gain a little experience in the form of test pieces. Obviously the agency pays you net of their commission, so expect slightly lower rates.

There are around 10,000 learned journals produced in Britain as well as several hundred specialist magazines. These are always subject-specific and usually highly technical, ranging in content from genetic engineering to the secret service. You don't have to be a technical expert to proofread (or even to copy-edit) papers for such journals, although any relevant experience you can offer will help. Drop a line to a few dozen editors and see how you get on. Journal editors are usually most insistent that their house style is followed meticulously, and journal style often differs from the accepted norms of copy-editing (for instance they may use double quotation marks instead of single for the British market or set mathematical variables in upright (roman) type instead of the usual italic). Take care!

We used the phrase 'British publishing companies' in the first sentence of this section, but you may wish to spread your net further. *Cassell's Directory of Publishing* lists publishers from all over the world, many of whom publish works in English and some of whom may well be seeking a freelance able to proofread and copy-edit in their mother tongue. English is the common business language of the European Union, and the current strengthening of European ties could well provide you with employment opportunities.

Whatever your approach to getting started, don't be depressed by rejection and don't give up. In my experience, it *will* be difficult, you *will* get there eventually, and it *will* all be worth it!

15 – 101 Potential Clients

There follows a list of 101 publishing companies who are documented as having contracted out work to freelances. You will find many more in the *Writers' and Artists' Yearbook*, *Cassell's Directory of Publishing*, *British Publishers and their Addresses*, *Willings Press Guide*, or one of the many other trade directories available at your main reference library. Also listed are the various imprints and divisions of these companies. (An imprint is a name under which a company publishes material usually directed at a certain sector of the market – for example, Penguin Books and Signet are both paperback imprints of the Penguin Group, but Penguin books are aimed at the 'discerning reader' while Signet titles have mass-market appeal.) The placing of freelance work for the various imprints and divisions of any particular publisher may be done by one person, or by different people each responsible for a particular imprint or division. Ask about this when you make your initial telephone call; it may be that one publisher can offer several freelance opportunities. Telephone and write to each one separately if this is the case – don't accept any kind offers to 'photocopy your CV and pass it round', however well meant. A brief note of the type of material published follows each entry. Fiction, non-fiction and science fiction have been abbreviated to f, nf and sf respectively. The category nf indicates that a range of non-fiction is published; if a publisher specializes in a particular field, more detail is given. The list comprises only a fraction of the freelance market, but it does provide a representative selection and should get you off to a good start. Company moves are frequent, so do telephone before writing.

AA Publishing Automobile Association, Fanum House, Basingstoke, Hants RG21 2EA; 01256 20123; *travel and leisure*

Abacus – *see Little, Brown and Co.*

Academic Press – *see Harcourt Brace and Co.*

Access Press – *see HarperCollins*

Addison-Wesley Finchampstead Road, Wokingham, Berks. RG11 2NZ; 01734 794000; *education and science*

Adlard Coles Nautical – *see A. & C. Black*

Anaya 3rd Floor, Strode House, 44–50 Osnaburgh Street, London NW1 3ND; 0171-383 2997; *arts and crafts, sport and leisure (see also Collins & Brown)*

Arkana – *see Penguin*

Armada – *see HarperCollins*

Arms & Armour – *see Cassell*

Arnold – *see Hodder Headline*

Arrow – *see Random House*

Bantam – *see Transworld*

Barrie & Jenkins – *see Random House*

Bartholomew – *see HarperCollins*

Batsford 583 Fulham Road, London SW6 5UA; 0171-471 1100; *nf*
  Seaby (imprint); *numismatics*

BBC Books Woodlands, 80 Wood Lane, London W12 0TT; 0181-576 2000; *TV and radio tie-ins*
  Network Books (imprint); *non-BBC tie-ins*
  BBC Educational Publishing Room A3148, Woodlands, 80 Wood Lane, London W12 0TT; 0181-576 2649; *educational*

Belitha Press – *see Collins & Brown*

David Bennett Books 23 Albion Road, St Albans, Herts. AL1 5EB; 01727 855878; *children's*

Berlitz Berlitz House, Peterley Road, Oxford OX4 2TX; 01865 747033; *travel and language*

Birnbaum – *see HarperCollins*

A. & C. Black 35 Bedford Row, London WC1R 4JH; 0171-242 0946; *children's, educational, nf*
  Adlard Coles Nautical (imprint); *nautical*
  Christopher Helm (imprint); *ornithology*

Black Lace – *see Virgin*

Black Swan – *see Transworld*

Blackie Academic and Professional – *see Chapman & Hall*

Blackie Children's Books – *see Penguin*

Blackwell 108 Cowley Road, Oxford OX4 1JF; 01865 791100; *nf*
  Shakespeare Head (imprint); *scholarly works*

Blackwell Science Osney Mead, Oxford OX2 0EL; 01865 206206; *scientific*

Blandford Press – *see Cassell*

Blueprint Monographs – *see Fourth Estate*

Bodley Head – *see Random House*

Bowker-Saur Maypole House, Maypole Road, East Grinstead, West Sussex RH19 1HH; 01342 330100; *biographies, directories, scientific*
  Hans Zell (imprint) PO Box 56, Oxford OX1 2SJ; 01865 511428; *reference, African studies, development studies*

Brassey's (UK) 33 John Street, London WC1N 2AT; 0171-753 7777; *military*
  Conway Maritime (imprint); *maritime*
  Putnam Aeronautical (imprint); *aeronautical*

Brimax – *see Reed*

Butterworth & Co. Halsbury House, 35 Chancery Lane, London WC2A 1EL; 0171-400 2500; *law, tax, accountancy*
  Butterworth Architecture (imprint); *architecture*
  Butterworth Law; *law*
  Butterworth Tax; *tax and accountancy*

Butterworth-Heinemann Linacre House, Jordan Hill, Oxford OX2 8DP; 01865 310366; *academic, technical, medical, business*
  Focal Press (imprint); *visual arts*

Cadogan Books Letts House, Parkgate Road, London SW11 4NQ; 0171-738 1961; *travel, chess, bridge*

Cambridge University Press The Edinburgh Building, Shaftesbury Road, Cambridge CB2 2RU; 01223 312393; *nf*

Jonathan Cape – *see Random House*

Frank Cass & Co. Newbury House, 890–900 Eastern Avenue, Newbury Park, Ilford, Essex IG2 7HH; 0181-599 8866; *nf*

  Vallentine Mitchell (imprint); *Jewish interest*

  Woburn Press (imprint); *educational*

Cassell plc Wellington House, 125 Strand, London WC2R 0BB; 0171-420 5555; *nf*

  Arms & Armour Press (imprint); *military*

  Blandford Press (imprint); *history, hobbies, music, New Age*

  Cassell (general imprint); *general nf*

  Cassell (academic imprint); *academic nf*

  Geoffrey Chapman (imprint); *religion*

  Victor Gollancz (imprint); *f, nf*

  Indigo (imprint); *f, nf*

  Mansell (imprint); *bibliographies, monographs, Islam, history*

  Mowbray (imprint); *religion*

  New Orchard (imprint); *nf*

  Pinter (imprint); *academic, professional*

  Studio Vista (imprint); *art*

  Tycooly (imprint); *environmental*

  Vista (imprint); *f*

  Ward Lock (imprint); *nf*

  Wisley (imprint); *gardening*

  H. F. & G. Witherby (imprint); *sport*

Century – *see Random House*

Chambers – *see Larousse*

Chapman & Hall 2–6 Boundary Row, London SE1N 8HN; 0171-865 0066; *scientific, technical and medical*

  Blackie Academic and Professional (imprint); *chemistry, food science*

  H. K. Lewis & Co. (imprint); *science, medical*

  E. & F. N. Spon (imprint); *architecture and planning*

Geoffrey Chapman – *see Cassell*

Paul Chapman 144 Liverpool Road, London N1 1LA; 0171-609 5315/6; *nf*

Chatto & Windus – *see Random House*

Clarendon Press – *see Oxford University Press*

T. & T. Clark 59 George Street, Edinburgh EH2 2LQ; 0131-225 4703; *law, philosophy, theology*

Collins – *see HarperCollins*

Collins & Brown Letts of London House, Great Eastern Wharf, Parkgate Road, London SW11 4NQ; 0171-924 2575; *nf*

  Anaya Collins & Brown (imprint); *nf*

  Belitha Press (imprint); *children's*

Condé Nast – *see Random House*

Conran Octopus – *see Reed*

Conway Maritime – *see Brassey's*

Corgi – *see Transworld*

Coronet – *see Hodder Headline*

The Crowood Press The Stable Block, Ramsbury, Marlborough, Wilts. SN8 2HR; 01672 20320; *sport, outdoor life*

  Helmsman (imprint); *nautical*

James Currey 54b Thornhill Square, London N1 1BE; 0171-609 9026; *Third World, nf*

Darton, Longman & Todd 1 Spencer Court, 140–142 Wandsworth High Street,
London SW18 4JJ; 0181-875 0155; *religion*

David & Charles Brunel House, Newton Abbot, Devon TQ12 4PU; 01626 61121;
illustrated nf, esp. crafts, hobbies & pastimes

André Deutsch 105–106 Great Russell Street, London WC1B 3LJ; 0171-580 2746; *f and nf*

Dinosaur – *see HarperCollins*

Doctor Who – *see Virgin*

Dorling Kindersley 9 Henrietta Street, Covent Garden, London WC2E 8PS;
0171-836 5411; *illustrated adult and children's nf*

Doubleday – *see Transworld*

Martin Dunitz The Livery House, 7–9 Pratt Street, London NW1 0AE; 0171-482 2202;
medical

Earthscan – *see Kogan Page*

Ebury Press – *see Random House*

Eclipse – *see HarperCollins*

Edinburgh University Press 22 George Square, Edinburgh EH8 9LF; 0131-650 4218; *nf*
  Polygon (imprint); *international f*

Edward Elgar Publishing 8 Lansdown Place, Cheltenham, Glos. GL50 2HU;
01242 226934; *economics, social sciences*

Elsevier Science The Boulevard, Langford Lane, Kidlington, Oxford OX5 1GB;
01865 843000; *science, technology, medical*
  Pergamon (imprint); *science, technology, medicine*

Lawrence Erlbaum – *see Taylor & Francis*

Faber & Faber 3 Queen Square, London WC1N 3AU; 0171-465 0045; *f, nf*

Fantail – *see Penguin*

Flamingo – *see HarperCollins*

Focal Press – *see Butterworth*

Fodor – *see Random House*

Folens Albert House, Apex Business Centre, Boscombe Road, Dunstable LU5 4RL;
01582 472788; *educational*

Fontana – *see HarperCollins*

W. Foulsham & Co. The Publishing House, Bennetts Close, Chippenham,
Berks. SL1 5AP; 01753 526769; *nf*
  Quantum (imprint); *philosophy, psychology*

Fount – *see HarperCollins*

Fourmat – *see Tolley*

Fourth Estate 6 Salem Road, London W2 4BU; 0171-727 8993; *f, nf*
  Blueprint Monographs (imprint); *architecture*
  Guardian Books (imprint); *Guardian newspaper tie-ins*

Freeway – *see Transworld*

Ginn & Co. – *see Reed*

Victor Gollancz – *see Cassell*

Gower Publishing Gower House, Croft Road, Aldershot, Hants GU11 3HR;
01252 331551; *management and business*

Graham & Trotman Sterling House, 66 Wilton Road, London SW1V 1DE;
0171-821 1123; *law, business, finance (published by Kluwer Law International)*

Guardian Books – *see Fourth Estate*

Guinness Publishing 33 London Road, Enfield, Middlesex EN2 6DJ; 0181-367 4567; *reference*

Robert Hale Clerkenwell House, 45–47 Clerkenwell Green, London EC1R 0HT; 0171-251 2661; *f, nf*

Hamish Hamilton – *see Penguin*

Hamlyn – *see Reed*

Harcourt Brace and Co. 24–28 Oval Road, London NW1 7DX; 0171-267 4466; *scientific and medical*

  Academic Press (division); *academic, reference*

  Baillière Tindall (division); *medical, veterinary*

  Holt, Rinehart & Winston (division); *educational*

  W. B. Saunders Co. (division); *scientific and medical*

HarperCollins 77–85 Fulham Palace Road, Hammersmith, London W6 8JB; 0181-741 7070; *f, nf*

  Access Press (imprint); *travel guides*

  Armada (imprint); *children's paperbacks*

  Birnbaum (imprint); *travel guides*

  Collins (imprint); *f, nf*

  Dinosaur (imprint); *children's*

  Eclipse (imprint); *graphic novels*

  Flamingo (imprint); *f, nf*

  Fontana (imprint); *paperback nf*

  Fount (imprint); *religion*

  Jets (imprint); *children's*

  Lions (imprint); *children's*

  Marshall Pickering (imprint); *religion*

  Nicholson (imprint); *maps and guides*

  Pandora Press (imprint); *nf*

  Thorsons (imprint); *medicine, self-help, New Age*

  Tolkien (imprint); *fantasy*

  Tracks (imprint); *children's*

Harrap 43–45 Annandale Street, Edinburgh EH7 4AZ; 0131-557 4571; *bilingual dictionaries*

Harvester Wheatsheaf – *see Paramount*

Headline – *see Hodder Headline*

Health Education Authority Hamilton House, Mabledon Place, London WC1H 9TX; 0171-413 1846; *health*

William Heinemann – *see Reed*

Christopher Helm – *see A. & C. Black*

Helmsman – *see The Crowood Press*

HMSO Books St Crispins, Duke Street, Norwich NR3 1PD; 01603 622211; *government publications*

Hobsons Publishing Bateman Street, Cambridge CB2 1LZ; 01223 354551; *careers, business*

Hodder Headline 338 Euston Road, London NW1 3BH; 0171-873 6000; *f, nf*

  Arnold (division); *humanities, science*

  Coronet (imprint); *paperback f and nf*

  Headline Books (division); *f, nf*

  Hodder & Stoughton (subsidiary); *f, nf*

  Knight (imprint); *children's*

New English Library (imprint); *f, nf*

Sceptre (imprint); *f, nf*

Hodder & Stoughton – *see Hodder Headline*

Hogarth Press – *see Random House*

Holt, Rinehart & Winston – *see Harcourt Brace & Co.*

Ellis Horwood – *see Taylor & Francis*

Hugo's Language Books Old Station Yard, Marlesford, Woodbridge, Suffolk IP13 0AG; 01728 746546; *language books and courses*

Hutchinson – *see Random House*

Indigo – *see Cassell*

IOP Publishing Techno House, Redcliffe Way, Bristol BS1 6NX; 01179 297481; *scientific*

Jets – *see HarperCollins*

Michael Joseph – *see Penguin*

Journeyman – *see Pluto*

Kingfisher – *see Larousse*

Kluwer Croner House, London Road, Kingston-upon-Thames, Surrey KT2 6SR; 0181-547 3333; *law, tax, business, medicine*

Knight *see Hodder Headline*

Charles Knight – *see Tolley*

Kogan Page 120 Pentonville Road, London N1 9JN; 0171-278 0433; *training, business, careers*

Earthscan (subsidiary); *Third World, environmental*

Larousse plc Elsley House, 24–30 Great Titchfield Street, London W1P 7AD; 0171-631 0878; and 43–45 Annandale Street, Edinburgh EH7 4AZ; 0131-557 4571; *reference, dictionaries*

Chambers (imprint); *reference, dictionaries*

Kingfisher (imprint); *children's*

Legend – *see Random House*

H. K. Lewis – *see Chapman & Hall*

Frances Lincoln 4 Torriano Mews, Torriano Avenue, London NW5 2RZ; 0171-284 4009; *nf, children's*

Lion Publishing plc Peter's Way, Sandy Lane West, Oxford OX4 5HG; 01865 747550; *Christian nf and children's*

Lions – *see HarperCollins*

Little, Brown and Co. (UK) Brettenham House, Lancaster Place, London WC2E 7EN; 0171-911 8000; *f, nf*

Abacus (division); *paperbacks*

Illustrated (division); *art, photographic*

Orbit (imprint); *sf, fantasy*

Virago (division); *women's issues, f*

Warner (division); *paperback f and nf*

Warner–Futura (imprint); *paperback crime*

Living and Learning Abbeygate House, East Road, Cambridge CB1 1DB; 01223 357788; *education, English, f, health, history, women's*

Longman Group Edinburgh Gate, Harlow, Essex CM20 2JE; 01279 426721; *nf*

Longman Education (imprint); *educational*

Longman ELT (imprint); *English language teaching*

Longman GeoInformation (imprint); *geographical*

Longman Higher Education (imprint); *academic*

Longman International Education (imprint); *educational, mainly for Africa, Caribbean and Middle East*

Longman Law, Tax and Finance (imprint); 21–27 Lamb's Conduit Street, London WC1N 3NJ; 0171-242 2548; *law, tax, finance*

Oliver & Boyd (imprint); *Scottish schoolbooks*

Macmillan Publishers 25 Eccleston Place, London SW1W 9NF; 0171-881 8000; *see divisions below*

The Macmillan Press (division) Houndmills, Basingstoke, Hants RG21 2XS; 01256 29242; *textbooks, reference*

Macmillan General Books (division); imprints include Pan, Papermac, Sidgwick & Jackson; *f, nf*

Macmillan Reference (division); *reference*

Macmillan Children's Books (division); *children's*

Picador (imprint of Macmillan General Books); *f, nf*

Macmillan Education (division) Houndmills, Basingstoke, Hants RG21 2XS; 01256 29242; *educational*

Julia MacRae – *see Random House*

Mainstream Publishing Co. 7 Albany Street, Edinburgh EH1 3UG; 0131-557 2959; *f, nf*

Mammoth – *see Reed*

Manchester University Press Oxford Road, Manchester M13 9PL; 0161-273 5530/5539; *nf*

Mandarin – *see Reed*

Mansell – *see Cassell*

Marshall Pickering *see HarperCollins*

McGraw-Hill Book Co. Europe McGraw-Hill House, Shoppenhangers Road, Maidenhead, Berks. SL6 2QL; 01628 23432; *science, technical, medical*

Mechanical Engineering Publications Northgate Avenue, Bury St Edmunds, Suffolk IP32 6BW; 01284 763277; *engineering*

Mermaid – *see Penguin*

Methuen – *see Reed*

Michelin Tyre plc Tourism Department, The Edward Hyde Building, 38 Clarendon Road, Watford, Herts. WD1 1SX; 01923 415000; *travel*

Minerva – *see Reed*

Mitchell Beazley – *see Reed*

Mowbray – *see Cassell*

John Murray 50 Albermarle Street, London W1X 4BD; 0171-493 4361; *nf, educational*

Thomas Nelson & Sons Nelson House, Mayfield Road, Walton-on-Thames, Surrey KT12 5PL; 01932 252211; *educational*

Nelson-Blackie Bishopbriggs, Glasgow G64 2NZ; 0141-772 2311; *educational*

Network Books – *see BBC Books*

New English Library – *see Hodder Headline*

New Orchard – *see Cassell*

Nexus – *see Virgin*

Nicholson – *see HarperCollins*

The Oleander Press 17 Stansgate Avenue, Cambridge CB2 2QZ; 01223 244688; *nf*

Oliver & Boyd – *see Longman*

Open University Press Celtic Court, 22 Ballmoor, Buckingham MK18 1XW; 01280 823388; *nf*

Optima – *see Random House*

Orbit – *see Little, Brown & Co.*

Osprey – *see Reed*

Oxford University Press Walton Street, Oxford OX2 6DP; 01865 56767; *nf*

  Clarendon Press (imprint); *academic*

Pan – *see Macmillan*

Pandora – *see HarperCollins*

Papermac – *see Macmillan*

Paramount Publishing Europe Campus 400, Maylands Avenue, Hemel Hempstead, Herts. HP2 7EZ; 01442 881900; *nf*

  Harvester Wheatsheaf (division); *humanities, literature*

  Prentice Hall (division); *science*

  Woodhead-Faulkner (division); *finance*

Partridge Press – *see Transworld*

Stanley Paul – *see Random House*

Pavilion Books 26 Upper Ground, London SE1 9PD; 0171-620 1666; *leisure, travel, sport, children's*

Pelham Books – *see Penguin*

Penguin Books 27 Wrights Lane, London W8 5TZ; 0171-416 3000; *f, nf*

  Allen Lane (imprint); *humanities*

  Arkana (imprint); *'mind, body and spirit'*

  Blackie Children's Books (imprint); *children's*

  Fantail (imprint); *children's*

  Hamish Hamilton (subsidiary); *f, nf*

  Michael Joseph (subsidiary); *f, nf*

  Mermaid (imprint of M. Joseph); *children's*

  Pelham Books (imprint of M. Joseph); *sport and leisure*

  Penguin (imprint); *adult paperbacks*

  Puffin (imprint); *children's paperbacks*

  RoC (imprint); *sf, fantasy*

  Signet (imprint); *mass-market paperbacks*

  Viking (imprint); *f, nf*

  Frederick Warne & Co. (subsidiary); *children's*

Pergamon – *see Elsevier Science*

Phaidon Press Regent's Wharf, All Saints Street, London N1 9PA; 0171-843 1000; *art*

George Philip – *see Reed*

Piatkus Books 5 Windmill Street, London W1P 1HF; 0171-631 0710; *f, women's, biography, self-help*

Picador – *see Macmillan*

Pimlico – *see Random House*

Pinter – *see Cassell*

Pitkin – *see Reed*

Pluto Publishing 345 Archway Road, London N6 5AA; 0181-348 2724; *social and political science, women's*

Pocket Books – *see Simon & Schuster*

Polity Press 65 Bridge Street, Cambridge CB2 1UR; 01223 324315; *nf*

Polygon – *see Edinburgh University Press*

Prentice Hall – *see Paramount*

Puffin – *see Penguin*

Putnam Aeronautical – *see Brassey's*

Quantum – *see W. Foulsham*

Random House UK 20 Vauxhall Bridge Road, London SW1V 2SA; 0171-973 9670; *f, nf*

  Arrow (imprint); *f, nf*

  Barrie & Jenkins (imprint of Ebury Press); *antiques, art*

  Jonathan Cape (imprint); *f, nf*

  Bodley Head (imprint of Jonathan Cape); *f, nf*

  Century (imprint); *f, biography, business, nf*

  Chatto & Windus (imprint); *f, nf*

  Hogarth Press (imprint of Chatto & Windus); *f, nf*

  Condé Nast Books (imprint of Ebury Press); *fashion, beauty, food*

  Fodor Guides (imprint); *travel guides*

  Hutchinson (imprint); *f, nf*

  Legend (imprint of Arrow); *sf, fantasy*

  Stanley Paul (imprint of Ebury Press); *leisure interests, dogs*

  Pimlico (imprint); *history, biography, literature*

  Random House Children's Books (division); publishes under Bodley Head Children's, Jonathan Cape Children's, Hutchinson's Children's, Julia MacRae, Red Fox, Tellastory; *children's*

  Rider (imprint of Ebury Press); *New Age*

  Vermilion, Optima (imprints of Ebury Press); *self-help, health, parenting*

  Vintage (imprint); *f, nf*

The Reader's Digest Association Berkeley Square House, Berkeley Square, London W1X 6AB; 0171-629 8144; *nf*

Red Fox – *see Random House*

Reed Books Michelin House, 81 Fulham Road, London SW3 6RB; 0171-581 9393; *f, nf*

  Brimax Books (imprint); *children's picture books*

  Conran Octopus (imprint); *lifestyle books*

  Hamlyn (imprint); *popular nf*

  Hamlyn Children's Reference (imprint); *children's reference*

  William Heinemann (imprint); *f, nf*

  Heinemann Young Books (imprint); *children's*

  Mammoth (imprint); *children's paperbacks*

  Mandarin (imprint); *paperback f and nf*

  Methuen (imprint); *f, nf, children's*

  Minerva (imprint); *literary paperback f and nf*

  Mitchell Beazley (imprint); *encyclopaedias, wine*

  Osprey (imprint); *military, automotive, natural history*

  George Philip (imprint); *maps, travel guides, astronomy*

  Pitkin Pictorials (imprint); *souvenir guides*

  Secker and Warburg (imprint); *literary f and nf*

  Sinclair-Stevenson (imprint); *f, nf*

Rider – *see Random House*

RoC – *see Penguin*

Routledge 11 New Fetter Lane, London EC4P 4EE; 0171-583 9855; *nf*

Royal National Institute for the Blind PO Box 173, Peterborough, Cambs. PE2 6WS; 01733 370777; *books in Braille and Moon embossed types*

Sage Publications 6 Bonhill Street, London EC2A 4PU; 0171-374 0645; *sociology, psychology, political and social science*

W. B. Saunders – *see Harcourt Brace & Co.*

Sceptre – *see Hodder Headline*

Scholastic Publications Villiers House, Clarendon Avenue, Leamington Spa, Warks. CV32 5PR; 01926 887799; *educational*

Seaby – *see B. T. Batsford*

Secker and Warburg – *see Reed*

Severn House Publishers 1st Floor, 9–15 High Street, Sutton, Surrey SM1 1DF; 0181-770 3930; *adult f*

Shakespeare Head – *see Blackwell*

Sheldon Press – *see Society for Promoting Christian Knowledge*

Sidgwick & Jackson – *see Macmillan*

Signet – *see Penguin*

Simon & Schuster West Garden Place, Kendal Street, London W2 2AQ; 0171-724 7577; *f, nf, reference, music, travel*

  Pocket Books (imprint); *mass-market paperbacks*

  Touchstone (imprint); *quality paperbacks*

Sinclair-Stevenson – *see Reed*

Society for Promoting Christian Knowledge Holy Trinity Church, Marylebone Road, London NW1 4DU; 0171-387 5282; *theology, medicine, business*

  Sheldon Press (imprint); *medicine, business*

  SPCK (imprint); *religion*

  Triangle (imprint); *religious paperbacks*

E. & F. N. Spon – *see Chapman & Hall*

Stevens and Sons – *see Sweet & Maxwell*

Studio Vista – *see Cassell*

Sutton Publishing Phoenix Mill, Far Thrupp, Stroud, Glos. GL5 2BU; 01453 731114; *nf*

Sweet & Maxwell 100 Avenue Road, London NW3 3PS; 0171-393 7000; *law*

  Stevens and Sons (imprint); *law*

Taylor & Francis 1 Gunpowder Square, London EC4A 3DE; 0171-583 0490; *educational science*

  Lawrence Erlbaum (division); *psychology*

  Ellis Horwood (division); *science*

Tellastory – *see Random House*

Thames and Hudson 30–34 Bloomsbury Street, London WC1B 3QP; 0171-636 5488; *literature, nf*

Stanley Thornes (Publishers) Ellenborough House, Wellington Street, Cheltenham, Glos. GL50 1YD; 01242 228888; *educational*

Thorsons – *see HarperCollins*

Tolkien – *see HarperCollins*

Tolley Publishing Co. Tolley House, 2 Addiscombe Road, Croydon, Surrey CR9 5AF; 0181-686 9141; *law, finance, business*

  Fourmat Publishing (division); *law*

  Charles Knight Publishing (division); *law*

Touchstone – *see Simon & Schuster*

Tracks – *see HarperCollins*

Transworld Publishers 61–63 Uxbridge Road, London W5 5SA; 0181–579 2652; *f, nf*
  Bantam (imprint); *paperback f and nf*
  Bantam Press (imprint); *f, nf*
  Bantam Young Adult (imprint); *young adult books*
  Black Swan (imprint); *paperback quality f*
  Corgi (imprint); *paperback f and nf*
  Doubleday (UK) (imprint); *f, nf, children's*
  Freeway (imprint); *young adult paperbacks*
  Partridge Press (imprint); *sport and leisure*
  Yearling (imprint); *children's paperbacks*
  Young Corgi (imprint); *children's paperbacks*

Triangle – *see Society for Promoting Christian Knowledge*

Tycooly Publishing – *see Cassell*

Usborne Publishing Usborne House, 83–85 Saffron Hill, London EC1N 8RT;
  0171-430 2800; *f, nf, children's*

Vallentine Mitchell – *see Frank Cass*

Vermilion – *see Random House*

Viking – *see Penguin*

Vintage – *see Random House*

Virago – *see Little, Brown*

Virgin Publishing 332 Ladbroke Grove, London W10 5AH; 0181-968 7554; *f, nf*
  Black Lace (imprint); *erotic fiction*
  Doctor Who (imprint); *Doctor Who tie-ins*
  Nexus (imprint); *erotic fiction for women*
  Virgin Books (imprint); *popular culture*

Vista – *see Cassell*

Ward Lock – *see Cassell*

Ward Lock Educational Co. 1 Christopher Road, East Grinstead,
  West Sussex RH19 3BT; 01342 318980; *educational*

Frederick Warne – *see Penguin*

Warner – *see Little, Brown & Co.*

Warner–Futura – *see Little, Brown & Co.*

Wayland (Publishers) 61–61a Western Road, Hove, East Sussex BN3 1JD; 01273 722561;
  children's nf

J. Whitaker & Sons 12 Dyott Street, London WC1A 1DF; 0171-836 8911; *reference*

Whurr Publishers 19b Compton Terrace, London N1 2UN; 0171-359 5979; *medical, business*

John Wiley & Sons Baffins Lane, Chichester, West Sussex PO19 1UD; 01243 779777;
  science, business, economics, finance, law

Wisley Handbooks – *see Cassell*

H. F. & G. Witherby – *see Cassell*

Woburn Press – *see Frank Cass*

Woodhead-Faulkner – *see Paramount*

Yale University Press 23 Pond Street, London NW3 2PN; 0171-431 4422; *nf*

Yearling – *see Transworld*

Young Corgi – *see Transworld*

Hans Zell – *see Bowker-Saur*

16 – Money Matters

If you have not been self-employed before you may feel a little daunted by the prospect of keeping your own books and dealing with the tax (wo)man. However, if you are organized and methodical enough to be a freelance, keeping your finances in order should hold no terrors for you.

Your jobcentre will be pleased to point you in the right direction, and the SFEP publish the Proceedings of their National Meeting on Tax and Accounting for Freelances under the title *The Tax Wo/man Cometh* at a very reasonable £3 or so. This will answer most of your questions, but if you still don't feel confident to handle matters yourself then find – preferably by word-of-mouth recommendation – a qualified bookkeeper or *small* accounting practice to assist you. Even medium-sized accountancy firms sometimes charge very high fees. You should be able to obtain competent, professional advice for a few pounds a week – ask for an estimate before agreeing to let anyone represent you.

Accountants charge by the hour, so the less work they have to do on your books the more reasonable will be their charges. Buy two A4 lever arch files, one for your invoices and one for your receipts. Number your invoices and receipts in consecutive series. You will also need a cash book to record payments into and withdrawals from your business bank account (do open a separate account for this, even if it's just a 'No. 2' account with your present bank or building society, otherwise you will find yourself in a dreadful muddle). Get into the habit of keeping your books up to date and you should not experience too many problems.

Ensure that you obtain, and keep, receipts for any purchases related to your work – pens, pencils, stationery, books, stamps. They all add up and they're all tax allowable! You will be able to claim a proportion of your telephone bill against tax and, if applicable, a proportion of your motoring expenses – keep *all* your petrol receipts, car parking tickets, garage bills, etc. and claim a suitable percentage of the total at the end of the year. You should also be able to claim a sum of around £8 per week against tax for 'use of home as office' if you are working from home full time.

One nice thing about being self-employed is that for the first couple of years or so you pay little or no tax. (This is because the Inland Revenue collect tax from the self-employed at least a year in arrears. Here is not the place to go into the ins and outs of tax returns and payment arrangements, but you will find full details in the free literature obtainable from your local TEC and the Inland Revenue.) The drawback is that when you are required to pay tax you must do so in a lump sum twice a year. You must, therefore, make provision for this by putting aside a proportion of your earnings – preferably in a high interest-bearing account.

The Inland Revenue have strict rules about what constitutes self-employment. If you spend more than about half your time working for any one client you may well be regarded as being employed by that client, even if your invoices are paid gross of income tax and national insurance. This creates problems for both you and your client: you may end up paying both employed and self-employed national insurance contributions and your client may also have to pay an employer's contribution on your fees.

The answer is to spread your net and build as wide a client base as possible. This is in any event desirable as the more clients you have the wider will be the variety of work you receive, and of course you will have fewer eggs in any one publisher's basket.

17 – . . . and Finally

It is said that a little learning is a dangerous thing, and it would be dangerous indeed to assume that the little learning you have gained from these pages and the exercises that follow is sufficient to turn you into a fully fledged proofreader and copy-editor.

However, if you can put into practice all that is contained here, you will demonstrate a mastery of the language far in excess of that exhibited by many authors and, in my experience, not a few professional proofreaders and copy-editors!

This is certainly enough to get you off to a good start, and I hope that you are sufficiently inspired to take the next step on the road to your new career. Remember, patience is a virtue; by following the advice given here I believe that you will succeed if you really want to – it's up to you.

Any comments or suggestions you may have regarding the contents of this guide will be read with interest, and of course we should be delighted to hear of your success.

Good luck!

Appendix 1: Proofreading Symbols

Listed below are some of the more common symbols used in proof correction. Extended lists will be found in *Copy Editing*, *Basic Editing* and the *Writers' and Artists' Yearbook*. Complete copies of BS5261 part 2: 1976 can be obtained from BSI, Linford Wood, Milton Keynes MK14 6LE, or (much cheaper) viewed at most main reference libraries.

Meaning	Textual Mark	Marginal Mark Old Style (BS1219)	Marginal Mark New Style (BS5261)
Delete	through letter or through letters		
Delete and close up	through letter or through letters		
Leave as printed	below letter(s)	stet	
Change to capital letters	below letter(s)	cap(s)	
Change to small capitals	below letter(s)	s.c.	
Change from caps to lower case	through letter(s)	l.c.	
Change to bold type	below letter(s)	bold	
Change to italic type	below letter(s)	ital	
Change to roman (upright) type	circle letter(s)	rom	
Change from bold to normal type	circle letter(s)	not bold	
Equalize space between letters/words	between letters	eq	
Delete space between letters	linking letters		
Reduce space between letters/words	between letters	less	
Insert space between letters	between letters		
Transpose matter	around matter	trs	
Begin new paragraph	around 1st word	n.p.	
Run on (no new paragraph)	linking words	r.o.	
*Insert new matter	between letters/words	(new matter)	(new matter)
*Replace matter	through letter or through letters	(new matter)	(new matter)
Move matter to left	around matter		
Move matter to right	around matter		
Wrong font (see Glossary)	circle letter(s)	w.f.	

Note: Although 'letters/words' are used above for convenience, the symbols are applicable to any printed matter (i.e. numbers, symbols, drawings, tables, etc.).
* Use the following forms in the margins: Full point⊙; colon⦂; apostrophe; quotation mark or ; exclamation mark(!); superscript , , etc.; subscript etc.; hyphen; en rule (dash).

Marked Example Using BS1219 Marks

One great advantage of freelancing is the ultimate flexibility it offers when it comes to choosing your hours of work.

You can freelance full time if you wish, or work just a couple of days a week or a few hours a day. you can work mornings, evenings and Nights if you want to and have a day off when ever you like (finances and and publishers' deadlines permitting). Its your choice

Marked Example Using BS5261 Marks

One great advantage of freelancing is the ultimate flexibility it offers when it comes to choosing your hours of work.

You can freelance full time if you wish, or work just a couple of days a week or a few hours a day. you can work mornings, evenings and Nights if you want to and have a day off when ever you like (finances and and publishers' deadlines permitting). Its your choice

Revised Proof

One great advantage of **freelancing** is the ultimate flexibility it offers when it comes to choosing your hours of work. You can freelance full time if you wish, or work just a couple of days a week or a few hours a day.

You can work mornings, evenings or nights if you want to and have a day off whenever you like (finances and publishers' deadlines permitting). It's *your* choice.

Appendix 2: 20 Common Errors

Here are some of the more frequently occurring categories of error – but you'll come across many more!

1. *Tautology* (saying the same thing twice): 'equally as good'; 'an essential prerequisite'; 'to revert back'.

2. Incorrect use of *either/or; neither/nor*: correct usage is 'either A or B' and 'neither A nor B'.

3. Incorrect placement of *both . . . and*: incorrect: 'The garden was attractive both in winter and summer'; correct: 'The garden was attractive in both winter and summer' or 'The garden was attractive both in winter and in summer'.

4. Incorrect use of *homophones* (similar-sounding words): 'discreet/discrete', 'affect/effect', etc.

5. *Missing punctuation*: beware of missing full stops, opening/closing quotation marks or parentheses.

6. *Double punctuation*: full stops both inside and outside closing parentheses/quotation marks etc.

7. *Wrongly ordered punctuation*: (Sentences completely enclosed within parentheses have their full stops before the closing one.) Sentences partly enclosed do not (as here). Commas, where used (as here), come after parentheses, never before. Question marks in speech should be placed correctly: Did you say 'It is ready'? He asked 'Is it ready?'

8. *Spelling errors*: preceeding (preceding); committment (commitment); satelite (satellite); ariel (aerial); embarass (embarrass); dessicate (desiccate); harrass (harass); etc.

9. *Inconsistency of spelling*: organise/recognize; focusing/focussed; etc. Use either form throughout but not a mixture of both.

10. *Inconsistency of presentation*: 'five boys ate 5 apples'; 'the team plays better when they are (it is) at home'.

11. *Hyphens in predicative compounds*: unless the meaning is unclear, hyphens need be used only in attributive compounds (i.e. 'the well-lit room', but 'the room was well lit'), and never following adverbs ending in -ly ('the newly arrived pupil').

12. *Inconsistency of hyphenation*: co-operate/cooperate; proofreader/proof-reader.

13. *Misplaced apostrophe*: none of the following needs an apostrophe: on it's own, his and her's, for two pin's, MOT's; the following should have the apostrophe before the 's': other peoples', each others', the childrens' clothes, the womens' group; the following are correct: in six months' time, Achilles' heel, the employers' association.

14. *Misuse of comparatives and superlatives*: comparatives (better, less, elder, higher) are used of one thing compared with one other: superlatives (best, least, eldest, highest) are used of one thing compared with two or more others: the nearer hill is the higher of the two, Robin is the eldest of the three.

15. *Misuse of words* (correct use in brackets): 'less' for 'fewer' (fewer cows give less milk); 'me and I' (goodbye from him and me, you and I have the same name); 'from and to' (different from, dissimilar to).

16. *Americanizations*: skeptical, analyze, paralyze, practice (verb), license (noun) in the USA; sceptical, analyse, paralyse, practise, licence in the UK. There are many other US/UK variations.

17. *Double letters*: targetted, combatting, skilfull, fullfil are all incorrect examples.

18. *Repetition*: It is not right for a writer to write the same word repeatedly right through a written sentence because he can't find the right written alternative. The writing written thus will be poorer than if the writer had done the right thing and written with the aid of a thesaurus, so avoiding the need for the piece of writing to be rewritten – right?

19. *Ambiguity*: 'The car was in the garage when he painted it' (painted what?).

20. *Letters incorrectly inserted or omitted* (keyboard errors): imminnent, particulary, hierarchial, verry, evry, etc.

Appendix 3: Contact Addresses

(Note: Although the following information was correct at the time of going to press, a confirmatory telephone call may be advisable prior to writing to ensure that addresses are current. Enclose a large stamped addressed envelope with any requests for information.)

The Society of Freelance Editors and Proofreaders
Mermaid House, 1 Mermaid Court, London SE1 1HR
Tel.: 0171-403 5141

The Society of Indexers
Mermaid House, 1 Mermaid Court, London SE1 1HR
Tel.: 0171-403 4947

The Translators' Association
84 Drayton Gardens, London SW10 9SB
Tel.: 0171-373 6642

The Association of Illustrators
1st Floor, 32–38 Saffron Hill, London EC1N 8FH
Tel.: 0171-831 7377

Master Photographers' Association
Hallmark House, 2 Beaumont Street, Darlington, Co. Durham DL1 5SZ
Tel.: 01325 356555

Bureau of Freelance Photographers
Focus House, 497 Green Lanes, London N13 4BP
Tel.: 0181-882 3315

The Scottish Book Centre
137 Dundee Street, Edinburgh EH11 1BG
Tel.: 0131-228 6866

Book House Training Centre
45 East Hill, Wandsworth, London SW18 2QZ
Tel.: 0181-874 2718

Ownbase (a support network for people working from home)
68 First Avenue, Bush Hill Park, Enfield, Middlesex EN1 1BN

Home Run (a magazine for people working from home)
Cribau Mill, Llanvair Discoed, Chepstow, Gwent NP6 6RD

Appendix 4: Proofreading Exercises

The exercises which follow are not proofreading tests in the normally accepted sense, since they do not involve reading against copy. It is a simple matter when reading against copy to decide whether a correction should be marked in blue or in red (see page 12), and I believe that the following fault-finding exercises, illustrating as they do some of the more common errors likely to be encountered, are a more valuable and clearer method of instruction in the black-and-white medium of this book.

Before you begin, read again the 20 common errors on pages 55–6 and the style guide below. Now read carefully through Exercise 1 and, on a separate sheet of paper, list as many errors as you can find. Use a dictionary to help you. Do not worry about the proofreading symbols at this stage and *do not write in the book yet*. Just jot down anything you feel is wrong, however minor. Now compare your list with the answers to Exercise 1 on page 69.

Don't be surprised or disappointed if you have failed to spot half of the errors or more – you are new to this, after all, and if you knew it all already there would have been little point in you buying this book, would there?

Work your way through Exercises 2 to 7 in the same way. Although the exercises are short, they each contain much for you to learn and you should not try to do them all at once. I would suggest that you spread them over a period of several days, and that you use the intervening time to analyse your strengths and weaknesses: if you missed several misspellings then you should make more use of your dictionary; if your grammar is poor you should be reading Fowler or Partridge (see page 28). Keep a note of your scores and then, after a few days' break, repeat the exercises. If you have learnt from your mistakes, your scores should be much improved. Remember, do not write in the book at this stage. When you feel that you have gained all you can from Exercises 1 to 7, and not before, proceed to Exercises 8 and 9. You may find it helpful to study the Glossary (pages 85–9) before commencing the exercises.

STYLE GUIDE

Exercises 1 to 7 should conform to the following style guidelines:
-ize endings
Dates: 1 May 1999
Numbers: spell out one to ten, otherwise use figures (but 5km, 8lb, etc.)
Thousands: 1,000; 10,000
Contractions: no points – Mr, Dr, Ltd
Acronyms: no points – USA, UK, RSPCA
Abbreviations: points – etc., i.e., e.g.
Quotation marks: single, double within single

EXERCISE 1

The final of the inter-village soccer challenge between Tidsham and Salton was a hard-fought affair. Tidsham set off at brakeneck speed, Bridges tearing down the left and easily beating the Salton defender Davies for pace before floating in a teasing cross which Brown headed just over the bar. Bridges's continuous crosses were a feature of the opening

5 ten-minute spell, posing a series of problems for Smith in the Salton gaol.

Despite Tidsham's early superiority, the first goal went to Salton when Smith's long clearance found Evans unmarked just outside the penalty area, the Welshman vollying an unstoppable shot past Parkes from 20 yards.

Their confidence boosted, Salton began to commence playing with more assurance,

10 adding a second goal after twenty minutes when Parkes failed to hold another Evans' thunderbolt and Taylor was on hand to stab the ball home from close-range to make the score 2–0.

Attention then focussed on the referee, the aptly-named Mr. Blewitt who awarded Tidsham a controversial penalty when the defender Davis was adjuged to have fouled

15 Brown inside the penalty-area, although the tackle seemed innoccuous enough to to most of those watching. Bridges duly converted the spot-kick and the score remained at two–one until half time, despite Bridges' continuing ariel bombardment from the right-wing to which Davies at right-back seemed to have no answer.

The weather worsened during the half-time interval, an Artic wind whipping up

20 snow flurries across the pitch. By the time the teams re-emerged the floodlights were on. The second half began at the same break-neck pace as the first, but this time it was Salton that looked the best team, Evans going close from a Johnson cross. Parkes performed miracles in the Tidsworth goal, his contribution proving indispensible in keeping the score at 2–1. A sense of *déja vu* was apparent when once again a goal came against the run of

25 play, Bridges again outpacing the pedestrian Davies to equalize at the near post

The Book of Revelations prophesies that the number of the Beast will be 666, but that prophesy must now be in question following the introduction of the Salton no. 12 – the hulking defender Arnold – as substitute for the hapless Davies. Arnold had made less than a half-dozen crunching tackles before his name was in the referees' notebook after a

30 particulary nasty foul on Brown, who limped out of the game with the assistance of two St John's Ambulance volunteers to be replaced by Bennett.

All Parkes's preceeding good work was undone ten minutes' from time when he fumbled an Evans shot and the ball slipped from his hands to roll agonizingly slowly into the Tidsham goal. Suitably chastised, despite his teamates' obvious sympathy, he urged his

35 team onto greater effort, but to no avail. They may have began the match as underdogs, but the Salton team was the most committed on the day and just about deserved their 3–2 victory.

EXERCISE 2

As a nurse in an old peoples' home I meet many interesting characters. Most of our residents are aged between 60–90 and none of them are without a tale to tell. One of my favourites is Captain Miller, who's repertoire includes several stories from the Second World War when he was a Captain in the Royal Navy. He's a typical navy man with a full beard and rolling gate, and its easy to imagine him barking orders to his crew from the bridge of *HMS Ironfist*. He says that the *Ironfist's* crew were among the best of World War II and that he was proud to be their captain. He captained three ships all together – the *Ironfist*, the *Hawk* and the *Andes*, the latter being one of the most advanced ships of its class. He would probably still be patrolling the high seas today if he hadn't been forced into early retirement due to an unforseen prostrate problem.

Mr Wilkes is an ex-boxer from Middlesborough. He was area champion from 1937–39, when the war interrupted his career. After the war he aquired a promotors' license and staged bouts all over the country. Mister Wilkes still takes a keen interest in the sport, but becomes most uncomplementary when comparing today's champions with his passed heros.

Mrs Rogers used to design wedding stationary. She still likes to practice and if I find a piece of paper covered in hearts and flowers then I know it's her's. Although confined to an electric wheelchair she is quite independant, often taking herself to buy pencils from the nearby newsagents shop and later showing us proudly what she has brought.

Our local cafe owner (who likes to describe himself as a restauranteur) lets us use his premises once a month for a tea-party and always provides a fine selection of goodies, including scones, éclairs and eccles cakes – Captain Millers' favourites. We used to organize pub lunches at the 'Red Lion', but had to cancel them when 3 lady residents were barred for invading the mens' toilets after over-indulging.

The home has beautiful gardens, and Mr Wilkes loves to lay in the sun when the weather is fine – he says it reminds him of his wartime days in Egypt – although whether he's serious or not is hard to guage.

Although poorly-renumerated, my job is a very rewarding occupation. I have been in the profession for fifteen years now, but each day still brings fresh challenges and great rewards. I would'nt swap it for anything!

EXERCISE 3

Wilham is a thriving town situated just this side of the Redshire–Bluesex border. It's
history is a long one, with signs of Roman ocupation from the period 49–6 BC. A hoard of
over 2,000 gold coins dating from that time and worth over £100,000 pounds was
discovered during the 1960s by a local man, Mr J.H. Osborne, who ensured that the whole
community benefitted from the find by funding a new wing for Wilham General Hospit-
al from the proceeds.

The town is dominated by two hills to the West, the highest of which – Saxon Hill, is
in fact man-made. Saxon hill is believed to be a burial mound constructed in about 650 AD.
At 432ft (132m) it is the highest in Redshire.

The plague years saw havoc wrought upon the population, which was reduced from
over 8,000 to 2150 in just 18 months during the sixteen-fifties. The parish records tell the
sad tale of a Mr A. F. Wyngate, who buried his wife and eight children in a 2-month
period. The evidence can still be seen in the grounds of the fifteenth-century St. Anselm's
Church with its imposing 150ft bell-tower. Equally as sad is the town's war memorial
which comemorates the dead of two world wars, many of who were between 17–21 years
old when they gave their lives.

Despite the ravages of both pestilence and of human folly, the town continues to carry on
flourishing in the 20th century. Wilham is fortuitous in being located near to some of the
county's best angling water, (a carp weighing over 40 lbs (18 kg) was caught in Wilham
Lake last year), which provides a major boost for tourism. The angling fraternity is
regularly targetted by the local tourist board in advertizing campaigns and many hotels
display 'Anglers Accomodated' signs.

Rambler's needs are also well catered for, with the lovely Wil valley just 5 miles
(8km) away. One victorian traveller described the River Wil as

> one of the prettiest to be found hereabouts, as any visitor will soon
>
> come to realise, with abundant fishes and other wild life . . . in such
>
> profusion as I have never before encountered. [The waters are] so clear
>
> that one may drink from them without fear of contaminasion (sic) by
>
> germs or diseases.'

It would perhaps be risky to follow that advice today, but the valley remains a
magnate for those seeking peace and solicitude.

EXERCISE 4

Satellite television has perhaps bought about the greatest advance in home entertainment this century. Within a period of a a few years viewing choice has been widened from just four terestrial TV channels to hundreds of stations. The choice is set to multiply still further with the advent of digital compression of programs which will mean that several different pictures can be broadcast simultaneously on the same channel rather than discreetly as at present.

Terestrial broadcasters are no doubt feeling under seige from the skies, though the BBC at least has siezed the bull by the horns and begun its own satelite operations, beaming programmes to the rest of Europe and beyond. It could be argued that it was the terestrial industry's use of satellite links that lead to the present situation, so it has only itself to blame. Others would say that we watch too much TV anyway and that the authorties should withold permission for any new channels.

With terestrial and satellite programme-makers competing for each others' audiences it might be expected that standards would have improved, but many are concerned that the opposite is true: the finite 'cake' being shared between more and more companies has resulted in lower-quality programmes each watched by less people.. There is also concern that Rupert Murdoch's communications empire, which comprises of several TV stations, newspapers, etc., weilds too much influence. Many wish that he had stayed in Australia, from whence he came, but even there he would be just a satellite link or two away.

200 or more channels to choose from but only one pair of eyes – how is the viewer to decide? Soccer or *Jurrassic Park*? Sky News or *The Simpsons*? The choice is not so hard as might be imagined. We have inferred that one must choose from between hundreds of channels, but most are not in our language and many are scrambled and officially unavailable to people in this country. This brings the choice for most of us down to a couple of dozen or so various different stations. We then need only to decide weather we in the mood for a film, news, travel, music, sport, childrens TV, etc and then chose one of the two or three channels devoted to our preference.

We may even end up listning to satellite radio instead, but thats another story all together . . .

EXERCISE 5

Natalie's heart rose as if on a ferris wheel when David walked into the room, his apparently disinterested dark-brown gaze surveying the assembled company and meeting hers for an instant.

'Do you know him?' asked Brigid.

5 'A bit. His Father has some horses with Daddy,' she explained.

'He works them occasionally.'

'I see', said Brigid, who had'nt taken her eyes off David. I wouldn't mind 10 minutes in the jacuzzi with him. Aren't you going to introduce me?'

But there was no need, for David was already making his way towards them through 10 the Halloween party crowd.

'Hello, I'm Brigid,' said Brigid, who was never slow off the mark.'

'Pleased to meet you,' he smiled. 'I'm David Manners.'

Natalie noticed that one of his front teeth was crooked. then she realised that she was staring and that he was watching her with amused interest. She flushed with embarassment.

15 'And I know you already, don't I?' David rescued her 'Natalie – Major Benson's little girl.'

'I'm eighteen,' protested Natalie indignantly.

'No offence meant.' He held up his hands. 'Just a figure of speech, that's all. I can see that your beautifully grown.

20 'I'm sorry, but you must excuse me,' he continued. 'There's a chap from the *Sporting Life* over there I want to see and then I really must speak to the major about *Egyptian Boy.* He'll win the Derby, Father reckons, maybe even the *Prix de l'Arc de Triomphe.*'

'Oh, Brigid, isnt he gorgeous,' breathed Natalie as they both watched Davids receding back. 'Did you see his eyes? They're the colour of cornflowers?'

25 'You could say gorgeous, I suppose, If you like the tall, dark, handsome, rugged type – which I do.'

Natalie looked crestfallen. He was sure to prefer Brigid's bubbly character and sexy looks. It had been that way ever since school: a continuing series of competitions which she won nine times out of ten. Brigid smiled avoraciously, oblivious to her friends feelings, 30 while Natalie silently conceeded defeat.

'There, that didn't take long.' David's voice interrupted Natalie's thoughts. 'Now then, Natalie, I wonder if you would do me the honour of accompanying me into dinner this evening. 'I feel that we should get to know each other better.'

'Close your mouth, Brigid,' said Natalie. 'The flies'll get in.'

35 She took David's arm, knowing instinctively that he had become part of her life forever.

EXERCISE 6

In its day the Radley Sabre was described as 'the car with the ultimate "going-power" '.[22] But did it have 'staying power?' Compared to the high-performance coupes of today the Sabre may appear pedestrian – indeed there are many family saloons with better performance figures – but it remains a favourite of enthusiasts. Many experts have poured over the Sabre's design; none, however have yet come up with a single overriding reason for the huge popularity of this sports-car phenomena.

James Radley founded Radley Motors on 31 November 1938 but, due to the Second World War, production was halted before it had really begun and the war years were spent fullfilling government orders for tank spares. Fortunately this delay did little to effect Radley's ultimate success and after a few months peacetime reorganization Radley Motors was back on course.

The first production model, the 'Dagger', achieved limited success. Competing for the same buyers as the Hillman Minx, it came second on nearly all counts.[23] The company might have folded there and then was it not for the vision of Radley's son-in-law and protégée Rupert Samson. Samson was convinced that the postwar world would produce a generation of young men with money to spare and young women ready to be impressed – as they already had been by the U.S. 'invasion'. Sampson's flair, (he was known as the Michaelangelo of car design) and Radley's engineering skills combined to produce the Sabre.

Whereas Radley's principle aim had been to provide value for money – a la Volkswagon – Samson's sole criteria was quite different to this. He thought that, if the product was sufficiently desirable enough, cost was irrelevant. 'Give 'em the best and they'll pay for it,' he is quoted as saying.[23] And he was proved right. During its first nine months' of production the Sabre, with its distinctive triangular radiator grill, became Britain's best-selling performance car, and for one breif period the best selling car in every category. [25]

It is all to easy to view such clasic cars with disdain from the comfort of their high-performance, fuel-efficient descendents, but in my view the Sabre and its designer is owed a debt of gratitude. Todays motorist may be spoilt for choice by the number of models on the fourcourt, but none of them are without at least a little of the Sabre in them – undoubtedly an irrefutable demonstration of 'staying power,' despite the fact that the last model rolled off the production line on the 17th of April 1967. Were it not for the Sabre, there would surely be far less models from which to choose today.

EXERCISE 7

The ending of a century always seems to concentrate mens' minds on the future, and never more so than today as we approach the millenium. No-one alive 100 years ago could have predicted the changes which have occurred during recent years. Even the futuristic writings of H. G. Welles from around the end of the eighteenth century could hardly be described as accurate (though one cannot read either *The Time Machine* nor *The War of the Worlds* with out experiencing a feeling of premonition.) George Orwell's *piece de resistance (1984)* comes closer, but even from his 1949 perspective he over-predicts the effect of state control.

There seems to be a paradox here; a contravention. On the one hand it seems that our forbears would find to-day's technology incredulous, yet on the other they over predict its effects! It seems that they are simultaneously overestimating and underestimating at the same time!

None the less, it is human nature to be curious about what lays ahead. What would today's generation find if they were transported to the 2090's? Computerization and miniaturisation are set to influence the future, so perhaps every household function from running a bath to walking the dog will be controlled by a miniscule box on the wall and a remote-controlled handset. It will probably be unneccesary to even be in the house so long as you had access to a videophone.

Shopping will be a thing of the past, with everything from a washing machine (will they still have washing machines?) to a Big Mac (there will surely still be MacDonald's!) available via the TV screen (which could well be a VR (for virtual reality) room by then.) Transport will be all electric, of course, and environmentally-friendly. AIDs and Cancer will be a thing of the past too (as will alzhiemers disease, cot deaths etc.)

In some ways its more fun to speculate on what *won't* have changed. 'Coronation Street' and 'East Enders' for a start; the National Lottery; no single european currency; lord Lucan still missing; and those shoes you want heeling will be ready next Thursday. Predicting is fun, but they shouldn't be taken too seriously. Look what happened to the last millennarians: the Norman Conquest took place just sixty-six years later. Let us hope that England's children have a less-traumatic time.

When you feel that you have gained all that you can from the fault-finding exercises, proceed to Exercise 8, which deals with the relative importance of the faults you have discovered.

EXERCISE 8

There is more to proofreading than simply spotting mistakes. Every blue correction you make will cost your client money. One publisher I work for told me that typesetters charge about one pound for every line in which a correction occurs, so if you mark three blues per page in a 500-page proof you will be adding £1,500 to that book's production costs. (*Note:* this discussion applies to blue corrections only, not red. See pages 11–12.)

It is therefore necessary to exercise a degree of judgement when marking blue corrections, deciding what to mark and what to overlook. This isn't easy. Different publishers have different standards; different people within the *same* publisher may have different standards; some books have larger budgets than others; some are more important than others. The simplest way round the problem is to mark everything, but to use pencil for 'borderline' corrections. This way the publisher has the choice of either inking in the correction or easily erasing it.

Borderline corrections might include a misplaced or missing comma or hyphen (so long as the sense of the sentence is unaffected), minor errors of grammar (so long as the meaning remains clear) and minor deviations from house style. Minor inconsistencies could also be ignored if they are not too glaring – for instance 'the Government' and 'the government' occurring on the same page would be unacceptable, but if one occurs on page 21 and the other on page 235 the publisher might not consider a correction worth while. For this reason, it is a good idea to add a helpful 'as p. 235' or 'as 2 lines earlier' next to the pencilled amendment to aid the publisher's decision.

Go through the answers to Exercises 1 to 7 and decide which are candidates for pencilled corrections, assuming that every correction is a 'blue'. Compare your list with the one on page 76. Remember, we are talking about judgement here, so there are no right or wrong answers.

Remember too that we are considering changes at *proof* stage, not at the copy-editing stage. The copy-editor would make *all* the changes if this were a manuscript, since cost would not then be a factor. We are just assuming that the copy-editor has done a particularly poor job and that all these errors have survived to the proof stage – a situation which is fortunately rare to this degree!

Note: author queries are not included in the list since these are never in anything but pencil. Use a separate sheet of paper to complete this exercise. Do not write in the book.

EXERCISE 9

Now you can write in the book! Mark up exercises 1 to 7 using the proofreading symbols shown on page 53. Use the new style BS5261 marks for the odd-numbered exercises and the old style BS1219 marks for the even-numbered ones. Marks relating to the left-hand half of each line go in the left-hand margin and vice versa. Use pencil for the borderline marks identified in Exercise 8 and make any appropriate marginal comments you feel would be helpful to the publisher (these must be as brief as possible without sacrificing clarity). Also mark any queries on the proofs in pencil. Then compare your marking with the marked examples on pages 77 to 83. All the circled marginal comments should be in pencil.

Warning: To gain maximum benefit from the foregoing exercises, you should avoid looking at the marked examples on pages 77 to 83 before you are ready to complete Exercise 9.

Answers to the Exercises

Figures in bold are line numbers.

ANSWERS TO EXERCISE 1

breakneck **(2)**; Bridges' **(4)** – the use of the possessive 's in words ending with s is a thorny problem (see *Hart's Rules* or *Copy Editing* for a full exposition), but the main thing to worry about at proof stage is consistency. The possessive s is omitted from Bridges' in line 18, and since the accepted convention is that single-syllable words ending with an *iz* sound should not take a second s, you should standardize on Bridges'; continual, not continuous **(4)** – 'continuous' implies an unbroken sequence, 'continual' a series of discrete events: a river flows continuously, a day's work may suffer continual interruption; goal **(5)**.

volleying **(7)**.

'began to commence' **(9)** is a tautology – either began or commenced will do; 20 minutes **(10)** – style; Evans **(10)** – no possessive apostrophe (change 'Evans' to 'Taylor', for example, and you will see that this is not a possessive case); close range **(11)** requires no hyphen since it is used predicatively (in simple terms, it is describing something earlier in the sentence – i.e. where the ball was stabbed home from). If used attributively (e.g. 'a close-range shot'), the hyphen would be correct.

focussed **(13)** is less common than focused, but the two are both correct and you should leave focussed, focussing, etc. if used consistently; aptly-named **(13)** needs no hyphen – most words ending in -ly are obvious adverbs and no clarifying hyphen is needed to join them to adjectives in compounds. Compare 'the well-named . . .' and 'the well named . . .': in the extreme case, the second could describe a well person who is named, or even a hole in the ground full of water! Adverbs such as aptly pose no such problems; Mr **(13)** – in British English contractions (i.e. shortened words beginning and ending with the same letters as the full words such as Mr, Mrs, Ltd, St) do not normally take full points, but abbreviations do (co., etc., e.g.). An exception to this rule is no. (number – a contraction of numero), which takes a full point to avoid confusion with the word 'no'. Some publishers prefer abbreviations without full points – always read the relevant house style guide and follow the instructions given; there should be a comma after Blewitt **(13)** to pair up with the one after 'referee'; Davis **(14)** should be Davies as throughout the piece; adjudged **(14)**; penalty-area **(15)** needs no hyphen (as in line 7); innocuous **(15)**; delete one of the two 'to's **(15)**; make two-one **(16)** 2–1 for consistency; half time **(17)** is OK, do not add a hyphen even though there is one in line 20 (see 'close range' above); aerial **(17)**; Bridges' bombardment is from the left-wing, not the right **(17)** (cf. line 2; also, Davies is at right-back so Bridges must be attacking down the left side).

Arctic **(19)**; re-emerged **(20)** is OK, so is reemerged, although it is usual to insert a hyphen where a double letter occurs. It is OK to vary style within the same piece (e.g. re-emerge and redefine) provided that any individual word is always presented in the same way. A hyphen must always be used if there is a likelihood of misinterpretation (e.g. re-creation and recreation do not mean the same thing); break-neck **(21)** and breakneck in line 2 should be made consistent; the better team **(22)** – there are only two teams so a comparative should be used, not a superlative (best applies to three or more); Tidsworth **(23)** should be Tidsham; indispensable **(23)**; *déjà vu* **(24)**; full point after post **(25)**.

Do not italicize books of the Bible **(26)**, but Revelation is correct (no s); prophecy **(27)** is the noun, prophesy the verb; no. 12 **(27)** is OK (see above); fewer than **(28)**; referee's **(29)**; particularly **(30)**; St John Ambulance **(30/31)** is correct (no s).

Parkes's **(32)** is OK – you do not have to make it consistent with Bridges' since it doesn't have an *iz* ending. You would, however, need to make Parkes's and Jones's, for example, consistent if both occurred in the same piece; preceding **(32)**; minutes **(32)** needs no apostrophe – if there were only one minute to go it would be one minute from time – not one minute's from time. You can use the same method to decide on two weeks' holiday a year (one week's holiday a year), in five minutes' time (in one minute's time), sentenced to six months (one month) in prison; chastise **(34)** is one of those verbs which never take an -ize ending (like advertise, circumcise, franchise, improvise, supervise, televise and several more), so you shouldn't have changed it, but you should also have realized that the word should have been 'chastened'– the next clause makes it clear that he was not chastised at all; teammates' **(34)** or team-mates'; on to and onto **(35)** are frequently used interchangeably, but onto is only permissible where there is a sense of position between two elements, one atop the other – he climbed onto the table. No such sense applies here, and on to is correct. On to is never wrong, but onto sometimes is. Several publishers do not permit onto in any circumstances – read house style guides carefully; begun **(35)**; 'was' **(36)** should be 'were' since 'team' has been used as a plural word throughout (there are no hard and fast rules about whether words such as team, government, committee should be treated as singular or plural nouns, but it is important to ensure that each such word is treated consistently throughout); more **(36)** – comparative.

ANSWERS TO EXERCISE 2

people **(1)** is a plural noun and its possessive is people's (similarly, men's, children's); between 60 and 90 **(2)** – 'between' should always have a corresponding 'and'; 'none of them is' **(2)** – none means 'not one' and it is the 'one' part to which the verb relates. This is singular, so should the verb be (similarly none . . . has). There are cases where the plural verb may be better – let common sense rule; whose **(3)**; a captain **(4)** – lower case c when used in a general sense (as line 7 below); gait **(5)**; it's easy **(5)** – remember, it's is only used for 'it is', not the possessive case; HMS *Ironfist* **(6)** – ships' names are always italicized, but any prefix (HMS, SS, MV, etc.) is always roman; the *Ironfist*'s **(6)** – similarly, the possessive 's is always roman when it follows an italic word (the *gendarme*'s hat, *Treasure Island*'s plot); World War II **(6/7)** – make this and Second World War in line 4 consistent (I prefer Second World War); all together **(7)** means all at the same time. Altogether is correct here, meaning in total; the latter **(8)** is only correct when referring to the second of two things. There are three ships, so 'the last' or 'the third' is correct; due to **(10)** in this context means 'caused by', owing to means 'because of'. Due to is wrong, owing to is better, but in this case the simple 'by' is best;

unforeseen **(10)**; prostate **(10)**.

Middlesbrough **(11)**; from 1937 to 1939 **(12)** – 'from' should always have a corresponding 'to'; acquired **(12)**; promoter's **(12)** (n.b. misspelling and misplaced apostrophe); licence **(13)** is the noun, license the verb (but license for both in the USA); contract Mister **(13)** to Mr as earlier and later; uncomplimentary **(14)** – look up the two versions in a dictionary if you are unsure of the difference; past **(15)**; heroes **(15)** is one of several words ending in o to take -oes in the plural, others are buffalo, calico, cargo, domino, echo, grotto, halo, mango, memento, mosquito, motto, Negro, portico, potato, tomato, tornado, torpedo and volcano. Some may be spelt either way – use a dictionary.

stationery **(16)** – stationary means still; to practise **(16)** is the verb, practice the noun (both practice in the USA); hers **(17)** – no possessive apostrophes with hers, its, theirs, yours, although 'one's own view' is correct; independent **(18)**; newsagent's shop **(19)**; bought **(19)**.

café **(20)**; restaurateur **(20)**; Eccles **(22)**; Miller's **(22)**; the Red Lion **(23)** needs no quotation marks – save these for song titles, chapter and article titles in reference lists, titles of poems. Similarly, house names – Green Gables, Dunroamin' – should be unquoted; spell out 3 **(23)** (style); men's **(24)**.

Hens lay **(25)** eggs – Mr Wilkes lies in the sun; the second dash (after Egypt **(26)**) should be a comma because all the words after 'fine' constitute a single idea; gauge **(27)**.

poorly **(28)** needs no hyphen (see Ex. 1); remunerated **(28)**; job and occupation **(28)** form a tautology – change occupation to 'one'; 15 years **(29)**; wouldn't **(30)**.

ANSWERS TO EXERCISE 3

'just this side' **(1)** is what is known as a parochialism – it means something to the writer but not to the reader. Query this with the author, who should change it to something more specific such as 'on the Redshire side'; It's **(1)** needs no apostrophe; occupation **(2)**; BC years should never be elided: it is unclear whether 49 BC to 46 BC or 49 BC to 6 BC is meant. Query with the author **(2)**; the £ sign **(3)** makes 'pounds' unnecessary; local **(4)** – wrong font; benefited **(5)**, although benefitted is permitted in the USA; Hospit-al is a bad word break **(5/6)**.

the West **(7)** usually only takes a capital when used to describe a political grouping (i.e. those countries with a Western culture), although this rule is not always observed so long as capitalization is consistent; higher **(7)** – comparative (see Ex. 1); use either a pair of commas or a pair of dashes round Saxon Hill, not one of each **(7)**; Saxon Hill **(8)**; AD 650 **(8)** – AD precedes the year, BC follows it.

2,150 **(11)** – all other 4-figure numbers in the piece have commas so this one should too (but not years of course); 1650s **(11)** – cf. 1960s in line 4 and be consistent – 1650s is less unwieldy. N.b. *never* use 1650's; A.F. Wyngate **(12)** – cf. J.H. Osborne in line 4 and make both sets of initials consistently spaced; two-month period **(12/13)** (style); St Anselm's **(13)** – no full point; include metric equivalent after 150ft **(14)**; 'Equally as' is a tautology **(14)** – delete 'as'; commemorate **(15)**; many of whom **(15)**; between 17 and 21 **(15)**.

Indent new para **(17)**; use either 'both of . . . and of . . .' or 'of both . . . and . . .' **(17)**; delete 'carry on' **(17)** – tautology; spell out 20th **(18)** to match 'fifteenth' in line 13 (the usual convention is to spell out centuries, but leave numbers if they are consistent);

fortuitous (18) means 'by chance'. Something which is fortuitous is not necessarily fortunate – the correct word here; delete comma before parenthesis (19) – the parenthesis provides the necessary break in rhythm and a comma is never used before one except in an embedded list, for example: we took (a) a tent, (b) a torch, (c) food for five days; 40lb (19) – never lbs; close up space in 18kg (19) – all other units in the piece are set close up, be consistent; last year (20) is another parochialism. Insert the correct year if known, query if not; targeted (21) is correct (in the USA too); ditto advertising (21); Accommodated (22); less space between 'Accommodated' and 'signs' (22).

Ramblers' (23); Victorian (24); do not change quoted matter (leave realise and wild life as they are (26); the ellipsis (. . .) indicates that some words have been omitted (26); the words in square brackets (27) are the author's interpolation – the author has replaced some of the quoted matter with some of his or her own and the square brackets indicate this fact to the reader. Author's interpolations must always be in square brackets; sic (28) means 'as written' and is used in quoted matter to indicate that such matter is reproduced correctly, even though it may appear otherwise. It is usually italicized, but you may leave roman if consistent. Since it is an interpolation, it should be within square brackets, not parentheses as here; because the quoted matter has been displayed as an extract, it needs no opening or closing quotes, so the closing quote should be deleted (29). (If an extract consists wholly or partly of direct speech, such speech should be enclosed in quotation marks as usual.); magnet (31); solitude (31).

ANSWERS TO EXERCISE 4

brought (1); delete one 'a' (2); terrestrial (3); programmes (4) – program is only used in Britain in connection with computers, as is disk; discretely (6).

Terrestrial (7); siege (7); seized (8); satellite (8); terrestrial (10); led (10); authorities (12); withhold (12).

terrestrial (13); each other's (13) – 'each other' is already a plural; 'might be expected' and 'would have improved' are not the same tense (14) – use either 'might have been expected' or, better, 'would improve'; 'between' indicates two dividing parties (15) – things are shared among several people but between two. We should also choose among several choices, but the use of between here is becoming so prevalent as to be considered idiomatic in some quarters; fewer people (16); delete second full point (16); things either comprise other things or consist of other things (17), so the Murdoch empire consists of several TV stations . . . Alternatively, the TV stations, newspapers, etc. comprise the Murdoch empire (though you would obviously make the former change at proof stage); wields (18); whence (19) means 'from where', so 'from whence' is a tautology – delete 'from'.

Irrespective of house style, sentences should never begin with figures – spell out 200 (20); *Jurassic Park* (21); roman '?' after *The Simpsons* (21) – only italicize punctuation if it relates solely to the italicized word(s) preceding it; infer/imply (22): an inference is a deduction made from other facts – we infer that the man the police are holding is guilty when the police state that they are not looking for anyone else in connection with the crime. An implication is a thing suggested, though not expressly asserted – by making the above statement, the police are implying that they think the man they are holding is guilty. We have neither inferred nor implied a TV channel choice – we have *stated* it;

delete 'from' **(22)** – it is redundant; among **(22)** – see above; three parochialisms in a row now (see Ex. 3): change 'our' **(23)** to 'the English', 'this country' **(24)** to Britain (not England) and 'of us' (24) to 'Britons'; various different (25) is a tautology – delete one; whether **(25)**; we are in **(25/26)**; children's **(26)**; insert point after etc **(26)**; choose **(26)**.

listening **(28)**; that's **(28)**; altogether **(28/29)**.

ANSWERS TO EXERCISE 5

a Ferris wheel **(1)** – proper noun; disinterested **(2)** – implies 'unaffected by the result, detached from' whereas uninterested means 'uncaring of the effects, nonchalant'. If a millionaire drops a pound, he may be uninterested in retrieving it, but he cannot be disinterested in the event because it has happened to *him*. David wants to appear uninterested; his father **(5)** should be lower case when used as a description. When used in place of a name (Daddy in the same line) the upper case initial is correct, for example: 'Father reckons' in line 22; run on: explained. 'He works them . . .' **(6)** – the same person is still talking; 'I see,' **(7)** – comma inside quote; hadn't **(7)**; insert opening quote before I wouldn't **(7)**; ten minutes **(7)**; Jacuzzi **(8)** – proper noun; Hallowe'en **(10)**; delete closing quote after mark **(11)**; capital T for Then **(13)**; realized **(13)** (style); embarrassment **(14)**; full point after her **(15)**; leave numbers spelt out in speech if consistent – eighteen **(17)** is OK; 'Just . . . that's all' **(18)** is a tautology, but should not be changed here since dialogue should reflect the way people speak, which is rarely grammatically precise; you're **(19)**; note that the 'missing' closing quote after grown **(19)** is correct since David's speech continues in the following paragraph; capital M for the Major **(21)**, which is used in place of the man's name (see Father/Daddy above); Egyptian Boy **(21)** – should be unquoted roman; proper nouns should never be italicized, even if they are foreign, thus Prix de l'Arc de Triomphe **(22)** should be roman (as should the Sorbonne, La Scala, Champs-Elysées, etc.); isn't **(23)**; put ? after gorgeous **(23)**; David's **(23)**; receding **(24)**; cornflowers **(24)** – his eyes are dark brown in line 2, cornflowers are blue – query with author; replace ? after cornflowers with full point **(24)**; full point after suppose **(25)** (or lower-case 'if'); which she won **(29)** – who? Change she to Brigid and query; avoraciously **(29)** should be either voraciously or avariciously – query which; oblivious **(29)** means heedless and, like heedless, should be followed by 'of', not 'to'; friend's **(29)**; conceded **(30)**; note the use of the comma before the vocative 'Natalie' **(32)** and also before Brigid in lines 23 and 34 – you should ensure that such commas are used either always or, if it is the author's style, not at all; put a ? after evening **(33)** and delete the opening quote which follows it; 'flies'll' **(34)** is fine in dialogue (see above) – do not change to flies will; forever **(36)** – means always, continuous or continual – the baby is forever crying, it was forever raining – for ever means until eternity, and is correct here. The two forms are often used interchangeably, but the difference is worth preserving.

ANSWERS TO EXERCISE 6

note use of double quotes within single around 'going power' **(1)** – the double-within-single convention is usual in the UK, but may be reversed in the USA. A quote-within-a-quote-within-a-quote would revert to single, and so on; 'staying power'? **(2)** – the ? applies to the sentence, not the quote, and so should follow the quotation mark;

compared to **(2)** means 'comparable to' whereas compared with means 'in comparison with' and is correct here. The two are often used interchangeably, but you should be alert to any possible confusion – for example, 'the chairman's wages could be compared to/compared with the company's annual profits' have two different meanings; coupés **(2)** is correct, though you could leave coupes if consistent; pored **(4)**; a comma should always follow however **(5)** unless used in the sense 'however hard we tried' etc.; none has **(5)** (see Ex. 2); phenomenon **(6)** – phenomena is plural.

30 days hath November . . . **(7)** – query; owing to **(7)** – (see Ex. 2); fulfilling **(9)** – n.b. to fulfil is the correct infinitive in the UK, fulfill in the USA; to effect **(9)** means to put into practice – affect is the correct word here; months' **(10)** (see Ex. 1).

Dagger **(12)** needs no quotes; were it not **(14)**; protégée **(15)** is feminine, protégé is correct here. There is no need to italicize if consistent. You may also find the accents omitted, which is acceptable at proof if consistent, though a regrettable fashion. Foreign words should always be italicized if there is an English equivalent which could result in confusion (e.g., the German *Land*, the French *place*). Similarly, accents must be added to confusible words (e.g. résumé is very different from resume). If a word is italicized, the accent(s) **must** be added, so protege is acceptable, but *protege* must be changed to *protégé*; US **(17)** – no points (style); Samson's **(17)**; no comma after flair **(17)** (see Ex. 3); Michelangelo **(18)**.

principal **(20)**; à la **(20)** – no need to italicize if consistent, but the accent is essential; Volkswagen **(21)**; criterion **(21)** – criteria is plural; different **(21)** should always be followed by 'from' in comparisons, never 'to', though 'dissimilar to' is correct; sufficiently . . . enough is a tautology **(22)** – delete one; irrelevant **(22)**; apostrophe before 'em **(22)**, not an opening quote; change note indicator 23 **(23)** to 24 – n.b., change the whole number, not just the 3 to a 4 otherwise you might end up with a note indicator 4 instead of 24; nine months **(23/24)**; grille **(24)** – a grill is used for cooking on; brief **(25)**; best-selling **(25)** – it has a hyphen earlier in the sentence; in any category **(25/26)** – it cannot be in more than one.

too easy **(27)**; classic **(27)**; there is no need to put a comma after fuel-efficient **(28)** but equally there would have been no need to delete one had it appeared there; descendants **(28)**; the Sabre and its designer (two things) are owed a debt, not 'is owed' **(28)** – another common error is to find one thing **or** another (i.e., a single thing) treated as a plural – for instance 'a cat or a dog make good pets' (makes a good pet is correct). Where you find a singular and a plural in an either/or sentence, the safest thing is to take your cue from the object nearest the verb, thus: 'His face or his hands are always dirty' but 'His hands or his face is always dirty'; Today's **(29)**; forecourt **(30)**; none of them is **(30)** . . . in it **(30)**; 'staying power', **(31)** – the comma relates to the whole sentence, not the quoted words, and should therefore follow the closing quote; 17 April 1967 **(32)** (style); fewer models **(33)**.

ANSWERS TO EXERCISE 7

men's **(1)** (see Ex. 2); this is also an example of gender bias – other examples are using 'he' to refer to a manager and 'she' to refer to a shop assistant. You will come across cures which are as bad as the disease: excessive use of 'he/she' or 'he or she', alternating use of 'he' and 'she' which can look very false, exclusive use of 'she' to compensate for years of male bias. Avoidance of either 'he' or 'she' is best; either make plural: the student and his books/the students and their books, or neutral: in the exercise, suggest 'people's' for 'men's', you can also sometimes use 'the' or a neutral pronoun such as 'its' or 'we' to overcome the problem; millennium (2); No one (2) should not have a hyphen; H. G. Wells (4); the nineteenth century (4); 'or' *The War of the Worlds*, not 'nor' (5) – the rule is either . . . or/neither . . . nor; without (6); premonition). (6) – the full stop applies to the whole sentence, not just the part in parentheses; *pièce de résistance* (6); the parentheses around *1984* should be roman (6) (the title of this novel is sometimes spelt out, but there is no need to change it if it has not been).

a contradiction, not a contravention (8); forbear means to abstain or desist from, and is sometimes found in place of forebear, meaning ancestor, which is correct here (9); today's (9) – no hyphen has been used elsewhere in the piece; incredible (9), not incredulous; over-predict (9) has a hyphen in line 7 and one should be added here; the two !s after effects (10) and time (11) are a bit much – I would query the first; 'It seems that' (10) has been used twice in quick succession – I would suggest deletion of the repetition; simultaneously . . . at the same time (10/11) is a tautology – delete one.

None the less (12) is often presented as nonetheless and used interchangeably with nevertheless, but there is a subtle difference as the sentence 'The meal was hastily prepared but good nevertheless, and none the less enjoyable for the cook's haste' illustrates. Ensure that none the less or nonetheless is used consistently throughout a set of proofs; what lies ahead (12) (see Ex. 2); 2090s (13) – no apostrophe; miniaturization (14) (style); minuscule (15); remote-control handset (16) – it is the box that is remote control*led* and the handset that does the controlling; unnecessary (16); to even be (16) is an example of a split infinitive (where a word is placed between the 'to' and the verb). Sometimes these are allowable if they are clearer than the alternative: 'he used the knife to finely slice the vegetables' is better than 'finely to slice' (which relates 'finely' to 'use', not to 'slice', which is intended) or 'to slice finely', which sounds ridiculous even though it is grammatically correct. To slice the vegetables finely is possible because 'finely' stays fairly close to 'slice', but if it were 'to slice the carrots together with cabbage, onions and fresh parsley finely' we could be in trouble! In the exercise, 'even to be' is the better alternative; It will (16) does not go with had (17) – change to have.

McDonald's (19) – the 'a' is often wrongly added and the apostrophe often wrongly omitted; note use of parentheses-within-parentheses around 'for virtual reality' (20) – in US books, square brackets [ ] may be used, but this convention is not usually applied in the UK so do not change here; the full stop after then (20) should be outside the parentheses; environmentally friendly (21) – no hyphen (see Ex. 1); AIDS or Aids (21); cancer (21) (no capital); things of the past (22) – there are two; Alzheimer's (22) – n.b., capital, spelling and apostrophe; insert a comma after cot deaths (22) – the rule is that etc. should be preceded by a comma unless it is the second of only two listed points, thus: 'reading, writing, etc. take up most of my time' but 'reading etc. takes up most of my time'. This rule is often ignored by (or perhaps unknown to) authors and copy-editors alike; insert full point after etc.) (22) – the one after etc. applies to etc. only, not to the whole sentence.

it's (23); TV programmes are sometimes quoted as here and sometimes italicized (23/24) – either is OK if consistent (cf. *The Simpsons* in Ex. 4. Book and film titles are always italicized); 'EastEnders' **(24)**; European **(24)**; Lord Lucan **(25)**; it shouldn't be . . . **(26)**; millenarians **(27)** – one n, but there are two in millennium, remember; 66 years **(27)** (style); Britain's children **(28)** – the use of England for Britain is especially favoured by American writers and guaranteed to anger non-English Britons!

ANSWERS TO EXERCISE 8

Exercise 1: continual **(4)**; close range **(11)**; aptly named **(13)**; better **(22)**; fewer **(28)**.

Exercise 2: is **(2)**; latter **(8)**; due to **(10)**; café **(20)**; Red Lion **(23)**; poorly- **(28)**; fifteen **(29)**.

Exercise 3: west **(7)**; higher **(7)**; AD **(8)**; A.F. **(12)**; both . . . and **(17)**; lb **(19)**.

Exercise 4: would improve **(14)**; among **(22)**; the English **(23)**; Britain **(24)**; Britons **(24)**.

Exercise 5: Ferris **(1)**; Jacuzzi **(8)**; Hallowe'en **(10)**; Major **(21)** (if consistent); oblivious of **(29)**; for ever **(36)**.

Exercise 6: compared to **(2)**; coupés **(2)**; none has **(5)**; owing to **(7)**; different from **(21)**; is . . . in it **(30)**. Note that I have not included fewer here **(33)**, even though I did in Ex. 1 above – it reads so much worse here, I think.

Exercise 7: No one **(2)**; forebear **(9)** (forbear is an accepted alternative in the *Oxford English Dictionary*); even to be **(16)**; environmentally friendly **(21)**; cot deaths, etc. **(22)**; 66 **(27)** (it is the only two-digit number in the piece); Britain **(28)**.

Remember, this is a subjective list of what might be considered the least-important corrections. Some publishers might ink in all of them, others none. You will learn which from experience.

Warning: To gain maximum benefit from the exercises you should avoid looking at the marked examples on the next seven pages before completing Exercise 9.

EXERCISE 1 CORRECTIONS – BS5261 marks

The final of the inter-village soccer challenge between Tidsham and Salton was a hard-fought affair. Tidsham set off at brakeneck speed, Bridges tearing down the left and easily beating the Salton defender Davies for pace before floating in a teasing cross which Brown headed just over the bar. Bridges's continubus crosses were a feature of the opening ten-minute spell, posing a series of problems for Smith in the Salton gaol.

Despite Tidsham's early superiority, the first goal went to Salton when Smith's long clearance found Evans unmarked just outside the penalty area, the Welshman vollying an unstoppable shot past Parkes from 20 yards.

Their confidence boosted, Salton began to commence playing with more assurance, adding a second goal after twenty minutes when Parkes failed to hold another Evans thunderbolt and Taylor was on hand to stab the ball home from close range to make the score 2–0.

Attention then focussed on the referee, the aptly named Mr Blewitt who awarded Tidsham a controversial penalty when the defender Davis was adjuged to have fouled Brown inside the penalty area, although the tackle seemed innocuous enough to to most of those watching. Bridges duly converted the spot-kick and the score remained at two-one until half time, despite Bridges' continuing ariel bombardment from the right-wing to which Davies at right-back seemed to have no answer.

The weather worsened during the half-time interval, an Artic wind whipping up snow flurries across the pitch. By the time the teams re-emerged the floodlights were on. The second half began at the same breakneck pace as the first, but this time it was Salton that looked the bett team, Evans going close from a Johnson cross. Parkes performed miracles in the Tidsworth goal, his contribution proving indispensble in keeping the score at 2–1. A sense of *déjà vu* was apparent when once again a goal came against the run of play, Bridges again outpacing the pedestrian Davies to equalize at the near post.

The Book of Revelations prophesies that the number of the Beast will be 666, but that prophecy must now be in question following the introduction of the Salton no. 12 – the hulking defender Arnold – as substitute for the hapless Davies. Arnold had made less than a half-dozen crunching tackles before his name was in the referees notebook after a particulary nasty foul on Brown, who limped out of the game with the assistance of two St Johns Ambulance volunteers to be replaced by Bennett.

All Parkes's preceeding good work was undone ten minutes from time when he fumbled an Evans shot and the ball slipped from his hands to roll agonizingly slowly into the Tidsham goal. Suitably chastised, despite his teamates' obvious sympathy, he urged his team onto greater effort, but to no avail. They may have began the match as underdogs, but the Salton team was the most committed on the day and just about deserved their 3–2 victory.

EXERCISE 2 CORRECTIONS – BS1219 marks

As a nurse in an old people's home I meet many interesting characters. Most of our residents are aged between 60–90 and none of them are without a tale to tell. One of my favourites is Captain Miller, whose repertoire includes several stories from the Second World War when he was a Captain in the Royal Navy. He's a typical navy man with a full beard and rolling gait, and its easy to imagine him barking orders to his crew from the bridge of HMS *Ironfist*. He says that the *Ironfist*'s crew were among the best of World War II and that he was proud to be their captain. He captained three ships all together – the *Ironfist*, the *Hawk* and the *Andes*, the latter being one of the most advanced ships of its class. He would probably still be patrolling the high seas today if he hadn't been forced into early retirement due to an unforseen prostrate problem.

Mr Wilkes is an ex-boxer from Middlesbrough. He was area champion from 1937–39, when the war interrupted his career. After the war he aquired a promotors license and staged bouts all over the country. Mister Wilkes still takes a keen interest in the sport, but becomes most uncomplimentary when comparing today's champions with his passed heros.

Mrs Rogers used to design wedding stationary. She still likes to practise and if I find a piece of paper covered in hearts and flowers then I know it's hers. Although confined to an electric wheelchair she is quite independant, often taking herself to buy pencils from the nearby newsagents shop and later showing us proudly what she has brought.

Our local café owner (who likes to describe himself as a restauranteur) lets us use his premises once a month for a tea-party and always provides a fine selection of goodies, including scones, éclairs and eccles cakes – Captain Millers favourites. We used to organize pub lunches at the Red Lion, but had to cancel them when 3 lady residents were barred for invading the mens toilets after over-indulging.

The home has beautiful gardens, and Mr Wilkes loves to lay in the sun when the weather is fine – he says it reminds him of his wartime days in Egypt although whether he's serious or not is hard to guage.

Although poorly renumerated, my job is a very rewarding occupation. I have been in the profession for fifteen years now, but each day still brings fresh challenges and great rewards. I wouldn't swap it for anything!

EXERCISE 3 CORRECTIONS – BS5261 marks

Wilham is a thriving town situated just this side of the Redshire–Bluesex border. It's history is a long one, with signs of Roman occupation from the period 49–6 BC. A hoard of over 2,000 gold coins dating from that time and worth over £100,000 pounds was discovered during the 1960s by a local man, Mr J.H. Osborne, who ensured that the whole community benefitted from the find by funding a new wing for Wilham General Hospit-al from the proceeds.

The town is dominated by two hills to the West, the highest of which – Saxon Hill is in fact man-made. Saxon hill is believed to be a burial mound constructed in about 650 AD. At 432ft (132m) it is the highest in Redshire.

The plague years saw havoc wrought upon the population, which was reduced from over 8,000 to 2,150 in just 18 months during the sixteen-fifties. The parish records tell the sad tale of a Mr A. F. Wyngate, who buried his wife and eight children in a 2-month period. The evidence can still be seen in the grounds of the fifteenth-century St Anselm's Church with its imposing 150ft bell-tower. Equally sad is the town's war memorial which commemorates the dead of two world wars, many of who were between 17–21 years old when they gave their lives.

Despite the ravages of both pestilence and human folly, the town continues to carry on flourishing in the 20th century. Wilham is fortuitous in being located near to some of the county's best angling water (a carp weighing over 40 lbs (18 kg) was caught in Wilham Lake last year, which provides a major boost for tourism. The angling fraternity is regularly targetted by the local tourist board in advertizing campaigns and many hotels display 'Anglers Accomodated' signs.

Ramblers needs are also well catered for, with the lovely Wil valley just 5 miles (8km) away. One victorian traveller described the River Wil as

> one of the prettiest to be found hereabouts, as any visitor will soon
> come to realise, with abundant fishes and other wild life . . . in such
> profusion as I have never before encountered. [The waters are] so clear
> that one may drink from them without fear of contaminasion [sic] by
> germs or diseases.

It would perhaps be risky to follow that advice today, but the valley remains a magnate for those seeking peace and solitude.

EXERCISE 4 CORRECTIONS – BS1219 marks

Satellite television has perhaps bought about the greatest advance in home entertainment this century. Within a period of a a few years viewing choice has been widened from just four terrestrial TV channels to hundreds of stations. The choice is set to multiply still further with the advent of digital compression of programs which will mean that several different pictures can be broadcast simultaneously on the same channel rather than discreetly as at present.

Terestrial broadcasters are no doubt feeling under siege from the skies, though the BBC at least has siezed the bull by the horns and begun its own satelite operations, beaming programmes to the rest of Europe and beyond. It could be argued that it was the terestrial industry's use of satellite links that lead to the present situation, so it has only itself to blame. Others would say that we watch too much TV anyway and that the authorties should withold permission for any new channels.

With terestrial and satellite programme-makers competing for each others audiences it might be expected that standards would have improved, but many are concerned that the opposite is true: the finite 'cake' being shared between more and more companies has resulted in lower-quality programmes each watched by less people. There is also concern that Rupert Murdoch's communications empire, which comprises of several TV stations, newspapers, etc., weilds too much influence. Many wish that he had stayed in Australia, from whence he came, but even there he would be just a satellite link or two away.

200 or more channels to choose from but only one pair of eyes – how is the viewer to decide? Soccer or *Jurrassic Park*? Sky News or *The Simpsons*? The choice is not so hard as might be imagined. We have inferred that one must choose from between hundreds of channels, but most are not in but language and many are scrambled and officially unavailable to people in this country. This brings the choice for most of us down to a couple of dozen or so various different stations. We then need only to decide weather we in the mood for a film, news, travel, music, sport, childrens TV, etc and then chose one of the two or three channels devoted to our preference.

We may even end up listning to satellite radio instead, but thats another story all together . . .

EXERCISE 5 CORRECTIONS – BS5261 marks

Natalie's heart rose as if on a ferris wheel when David walked into the room, his apparently disinterested dark-brown gaze surveying the assembled company and meeting hers for an instant.

'Do you know him?' asked Brigid.

'A bit. His Father has some horses with Daddy,' she explained. 'He works them occasionally.'

'I see,' said Brigid, who hadn't taken her eyes off David. 'I wouldn't mind ten minutes in the jacuzzi with him. Aren't you going to introduce me?'

But there was no need, for David was already making his way towards them through the Halloween party crowd.

'Hello, I'm Brigid,' said Brigid, who was never slow off the mark.

'Pleased to meet you,' he smiled. 'I'm David Manners.'

Natalie noticed that one of his front teeth was crooked. then she realised that she was staring and that he was watching her with amused interest. She flushed with embarassment.

'And I know you already, don't I?' David rescued her 'Natalie – Major Benson's little girl.'

'I'm eighteen,' protested Natalie indignantly.

'No offence meant.' He held up his hands. 'Just a figure of speech, that's all. I can see that you beautifully grown.

'I'm sorry, but you must excuse me,' he continued. 'There's a chap from the *Sporting Life* over there I want to see and then I really must speak to the major about *Egyptian Boy*. He'll win the Derby, Father reckons, maybe even the *Prix de l'Arc de Triomphe.*

'Oh, Brigid, isnt he gorgeous' breathed Natalie as they both watched David's receeding back. 'Did you see his eyes? They're the colour of cornflowers.'

'You could say gorgeous, I suppose If you like the tall, dark, handsome, rugged type – which I do.'

Natalie looked crestfallen. He was sure to prefer Brigid's bubbly character and sexy looks. It had been that way ever since school: a continuing series of competitions which she won nine times out of ten. Brigid smiled voraciously, oblivious to her friends feelings, while Natalie silently conceeded defeat.

'There, that didn't take long.' David's voice interrupted Natalie's thoughts. 'Now then, Natalie, I wonder if you would do me the honour of accompanying me into dinner this evening I feel that we should get to know each other better.'

'Close your mouth, Brigid,' said Natalie. 'The flies'll get in.'

She took David's arm, knowing instinctively that he had become part of her life forever.

EXERCISE 6 CORRECTIONS – BS1219 marks

In its day the Radley Sabre was described as 'the car with the ultimate "going-power" '.[22] But did it have 'staying power'? Compared to the high-performance coupés of today the Sabre may appear pedestrian – indeed there are many family saloons with better performance figures – but it remains a favourite of enthusiasts. Many experts have pored over the Sabre's design; none, however, have yet come up with a single overriding reason for the huge popularity of this sports-car phenomenon.

James Radley founded Radley Motors on 31 November 1938 but, owing to the Second World War, production was halted before it had really begun and the war years were spent fulfilling government orders for tank spares. Fortunately this delay did little to affect Radley's ultimate success and after a few months' peacetime reorganization Radley Motors was back on course.

The first production model, the Dagger, achieved limited success. Competing for the same buyers as the Hillman Minx, it came second on nearly all counts.[23] The company might have folded there and then were it not for the vision of Radley's son-in-law and protégé Rupert Samson. Samson was convinced that the postwar world would produce a generation of young men with money to spare and young women ready to be impressed – as they already had been by the US 'invasion'. Samson's flair (he was known as the Michaelangelo of car design) and Radley's engineering skills combined to produce the Sabre.

Whereas Radley's principal aim had been to provide value for money – à la Volkswagen – Samson's sole criterion was quite different from this. He thought that, if the product was sufficiently desirable, cost was irrelevant. 'Give 'em the best and they'll pay for it,' he is quoted as saying.[24] And he was proved right. During its first nine months of production the Sabre, with its distinctive triangular radiator grille, became Britain's best-selling performance car, and for one brief period the best-selling car in any category.[25]

It is all too easy to view such classic cars with disdain from the comfort of their high-performance, fuel-efficient descendants, but in my view the Sabre and its designer are owed a debt of gratitude. Today's motorist may be spoilt for choice by the number of models on the forecourt, but none of them is without at least a little of the Sabre in it – undoubtedly an irrefutable demonstration of 'staying power' despite the fact that the last model rolled off the production line on 17 April 1967. Were it not for the Sabre, there would surely be far fewer models from which to choose today.

EXERCISE 7 CORRECTIONS – BS5261 marks

The ending of a century always seems to concentrate mens' minds on the future, and never more so than today as we approach the millenium. No one alive 100 years ago could have predicted the changes which have occurred during recent years. Even the futuristic writings of H. G. Welles from around the end of the eighteenth century could hardly be described as accurate (though one cannot read either *The Time Machine* nor *The War of the Worlds* without experiencing a feeling of premonition) George Orwell's *pièce de résistance* (1984) comes closer, but even from his 1949 perspective he over-predicts the effect of state control.

There seems to be a paradox here; a contravention. On the one hand it seems that our forbears would find to day's technology incredulous, yet on the other they over/predict its effects. It seems that they are simultaneously overestimating and underestimating at the same time!

None the less, it is human nature to be curious about what lays ahead. What would today's generation find if they were transported to the 2090's? Computerization and miniaturisation are set to influence the future, so perhaps every household function from running a bath to walking the dog will be controlled by a minuscule box on the wall and a remote-controlled handset. It will probably be unnecesary to even be in the house so long as you had access to a videophone.

Shopping will be a thing of the past, with everything from a washing machine (will they still have washing machines?) to a Big Mac (there will surely still be MacDonald's!) available via the TV screen (which could well be a VR (for virtual reality) room by then) Transport will be all electric, of course, and environmentally friendly. AIDs and Cancer will be a thing of the past too (as will alzhiemers disease, cot deaths etc.)

In some ways its more fun to speculate on what *won't* have changed. 'Coronation Street' and 'East Enders' for a start; the National Lottery; no single european currency; lord Lucan still missing; and those shoes you want heeling will be ready next Thursday. Predicting is fun, but they shouldn't be taken too seriously. Look what happened to the last millenarians: the Norman Conquest took place just sixty-six years later. Let us hope that England's children have a less-traumatic time.

repetition – cf. l.8 – delete?

Glossary

Note: Italicized words have separate glossary entries.

arabic numerals	The numerals 0 to 9.
artwork	Drawings, figures, graphs, etc. for reproduction.
author-date system	A system of referring to *references* in the text using the author and the year of publication – for instance, this book would be Horwood (1995). A list of references in full would be found either at the end of each chapter or at the end of the book.
a/w	Abbreviation of *artwork*.
bad break	An inelegant or misleading *word break*.
bibliography	A list of published material relevant to the text, but not necessarily used as source material (cf. *references*).
blurb	A brief description of the book, usually found on the jacket, flyleaf, *quarter-title page* or *half-title page*.
bracket	A square bracket] or [(cf. *parenthesis*).
bullet point	A large dot used before list items.
camera-ready copy	Material ready for reproduction in its final form.
cap(s)	Capital letter(s).
caption	The words describing a picture, drawing, figure, etc.; typeset separately from the text.
cf.	'Compare', from the Latin *confer*. It does *not* mean 'see'.
chapter head	The title of a chapter, often abbreviated to Ch. hd.
collation	The transferring of corrections from more than one set of *proofs* on to the *marked set*.
colophon	A publisher's logo.
c.r.c.	Abbreviation of *camera-ready copy*.
depth	see *page depth*.
diacritical marks	Accents, dots, bars, etc. above or below letters.
diaresis	Two dots placed above a vowel to modify its pronunciation: naïve, Citroën, etc.
display	An instruction to present copy in such a way as to distinguish it from the rest of the text.
electronic typescript	A *typescript* prepared on a computer disk.
elision	The running together of numbers, e.g. pages 122–123 may be elided to pages 122–3. *En rules* are normally used for elision.
ellipsis	A series of (usually three) dots used to indicate missing words in an *extract*. The plural is ellipses.
em	The width of a capital letter M – the width will depend on the *font* and the *point size*.
em rule	A *rule* of length one *em*.
embedded	Included in the *typescript* rather than provided on a separate sheet.
en	Half an *em*.

en rule	A *rule* half the length of an *em rule*. En rules with a space either side (spaced en rules) are usually used for dashes.
endmatter	Copy following the main text.
endnotes	Explanatory notes found either at the end of a chapter or at the end of a book.
epigraph	A quotation usually found at the beginning of a book or chapter.
e.t.s.	Abbreviation of *electronic typescript*.
extent	The length of a book or *typescript*. May be given in number of pages or number of words.
extract	A quotation, often *displayed* by using indentation or a smaller *point size*.
flag	A small piece of paper, often a Post-It note, placed in the *typescript* to draw attention to one or more *folios* (for example, to indicate the position of *artwork*).
folio	(i) a page of a **typescript**, (ii) a page number in a book, (iii) a term used to indicate the size of a book (in the same vein as quarto, octavo, etc.).
follow on	A copy-editorial instruction meaning 'do not leave any extra space here'.
font	Any specific style and *point size* of lettering or type. Also known as fount.
footnote	A note appearing at the foot of a page.
foreword	An introduction to a book, usually written by someone other than the author.
foul proof	A set of *proofs* which have been corrected by the typesetter and are no longer required. When the *marked proof* is returned from the typesetter together with the *revise proof*, the marked set becomes the foul proof.
fount	see *font*.
fresh page	A copy-editorial instruction to the typesetter to start a new page. May be fresh *recto* or fresh *verso* if the material has to begin on a recto or verso page (for example, the contents page and the first page of the first chapter in most books begin on a fresh recto).
full out	Aligned with the text width margins, more often associated with the left-hand margin.
full point	A full stop.
galley proof	A *proof* which has not been sectioned into pages.
global correction	An instruction input on to a computer disk containing a *typescript*, which will amend every occurrence of the word concerned.
half-title page	The *recto* page preceding the *title page*.
halftone	A black-and-white illustration where shades of grey are produced by using varying concentrations of dots.
hard copy	The paper printout from a computer.
Harvard system	A referencing system virtually identical to the *author-date system*. The two terms are often used interchangeably.
headline	Another term for *running head*.
house style	The style of presentation to which a publishing company wishes its books to conform.

ibid., ibidem	'In the same place'. Used in notes to indicate the same source as quoted immediately before.
idem, id.	'The same'. Used to mean 'by the same author as has just been referred to'. The female version is *eadem*.
imprint	The name under which a publisher publishes.
imprints page	The page containing the publisher's *imprint* and other library cataloguing information. Usually found on the *verso* following the *title page*.
indicator	A *superscript* letter, number or symbol in the text indicating that a *footnote* or an *endnote* should be consulted at this point.
ISBN	International Standard Book Number. Every book has a unique ISBN.
justified	With the right and left edges of each line aligned.
landscape	An illustration or table turned on its side with its bottom edge facing to the right (cf. *portrait*).
l.c.	Abbreviation of *lower case*.
ligature	Two or more letters joined to make a single character, e.g. œ, æ, Æ, Œ, etc.
line drawing	A drawing consisting only of lines and shading with no *halftones*.
lining figures	*Arabic numerals* where the bottom of each numeral sits on the line of text (cf. *non-lining figures*).
list comma	see *serial comma*.
literal	A mistake in *typesetting* such as a wrongly inserted or omitted character.
loc. cit.	'In the place cited'. Used in notes.
long page	A page containing more lines than the correct *page depth*.
lower case	Small letters, not capitals.
make-up	The composition of a page of text.
manuscript	The original handwritten or typed version of a book submitted to a publisher by an author. In practice, nowadays, it usually means the same as *typescript*.
marginal mark	Mark made in the margin by proofreader to indicate to the typesetter that a correction is required.
marked proof	A *proof* which has been corrected by a proofreader reading against copy. Author's corrections and, if applicable, corrections from proofs which have been read blind are added to the marked proof during *collation*. Also known as marked set.
non-lining figures	*Arabic numerals* which do not all sit on the line of text, the numbers 3, 4, 5, 7 and 9 descending below the line and the numbers 6 and 8 rising higher than 0, 1 and 2.
note indicator	see *indicator*.
old-style figures	*Non-lining figures*.
op. cit.	'In the work cited'. Used in notes.
original	An original piece of *artwork* as supplied by the author.
orphan	The first line of a paragraph occurring on the last line of a page. See also *widow*.
page depth	The vertical measure of the text on a page.
page proofs	*Proofs* produced in looseleaf form with page numbers inserted.
pagehead	Another term for *running head*.

pagination	The numbering of pages.
parenthesis	A round bracket) or (. Often abbreviated to paren. The plural is parentheses. See also *bracket*.
part title	The title of a group of chapters forming part of a book. The part title usually appears on its own on a fresh *recto* known as the part-title page.
passim	Latin word meaning 'At various places throughout the text'.
paste-up	Using *galley proofs* and *artwork* to *make-up* pages.
point size	The size of the letters in any particular style of type. Based on the capital M of a *font*, there are approximately 72 points to the inch, thus the M of a 12-point font is approximately one-sixth of an inch high.
portrait	An illustration or table set upright on the page (cf. *landscape*).
preface	An introductory section, usually written by the author.
preliminary pages	That part of a book preceding the first chapter.
prime	The mathematical notation ′, used in 6′6″ etc.
proof	A *typescript* which has been typeset in looseleaf form.
quarter-title page	The *recto* page preceding the *half-title page*.
quotes	Quotation marks. May be 'single' or "double".
ragged right	Form of *typesetting* where the right-hand edges of each line are not aligned.
range	Align. Thus the instruction 'range left' means that the first letters of every line should align, the instruction 'range right' that the final letters of every line should align.
recto	The right-hand page of a *spread*.
references	Sources used in preparing a book, chapter or article and listed at the end of the book, chapter or article.
revise proof	Set of *proofs* which have been corrected by the typesetter.
R/L	Abbreviation of range left (see *range*).
rough	A piece of *artwork* requiring correction or redrawing.
R/R or R/Rt	Abbreviation of range right (see *range*).
rule	A solid horizontal line. May be anything from one en long (*en rule*) to the full width of the page.
run on or r.o.	Do not begin a new line.
running head	Words at the top of a page. May be the book title, chapter title, *section* title or chapter author.
s.c.	Abbreviation of small capitals.
section	A division of a chapter.
section head	A *section*'s title.
serial comma	The comma preceding 'and' in a list of three or more items, also known as a list comma. Serial commas should be either consistently included (red, white, and blue) or consistently omitted (red, white and blue) throughout – it doesn't matter which unless your publisher specifies a preference in their house style. American authors use serial commas more often than British authors do. This would definitely be a 'pencilled' correction at proof stage (see Exercise 8) unless two inconsistent lists are very close together.
short page	A page containing fewer lines than the correct *page depth*.

short-title system   A system of citing *references* in the text in which the title of a source is given in full at first mention and an abbreviated version used for subsequent citations; for instance, this book might be referred to as Horwood, *Freelance*.

size down   An instruction to use a smaller *point size*.

small caps   Small capital letters. Small caps should be used where *cap(s)* occur adjacent to *non-lining figures* (e.g. in postcodes).

solidus   An oblique stroke: /.

sort   An individual letter or character.

special sort   A *sort* which is out of the ordinary, for example, a Greek letter, a special mathematical symbol, etc.

spread   Two facing pages, *verso* and *recto*.

stet   'Let it stand'. Used to instruct the typesetter to ignore a change which has been made in error.

subscript   A *sized-down* figure or letter following and/or below the level of a full-sized one, e.g. the '2' in H_2O.

subsection   A division of a *section*.

superscript   A *sized-down* figure or letter following and/or above the level of a full-sized one. *Indicators* for notes are set in superscript.

textual mark   Mark made in the text by a proofreader to indicate to the typesetter that a correction is required.

tilde   The wavy line sometimes found above the letter ñ in Spanish words.

title page   *Recto* page near the front of the book containing the book's title in full.

typescript   Copy supplied by an author. May be typewritten, *hard copy* or *electronic*.

typesetting   The setting of a *typescript* using one or more specified *fonts*.

typo or **typographical error**   A mistake in *typesetting* which is not a *literal*, such as using the wrong *font* or setting to an incorrect *page depth*.

u.c.   Abbreviation of *upper case*.

umlaut   A German accent similar in appearance to a *diaresis*, i.e. ö, ü, ë. Used on both upper and lower case letters (unlike French accents, which are often omitted above upper case letters).

upper case   Capital (letters).

verso   The left-hand page of a *spread*.

w.f.   Abbreviation of wrong *font*.

widow   The last line of a paragraph when it appears as the first line of a page. Publishers are usually anxious to avoid widows, especially if they are less than three-quarters of a line long, but less bothered about *orphans*.

word break   The division of a word at the end of a line using a hyphen.

Bibliography

Copy-editing and Proofreading

Butcher, Judith, *Copy-editing* (3rd edn), Cambridge: Cambridge University Press
Chicago Manual of Style (14th edn), Chicago: University of Chicago Press (American style guide)
Economist Style Guide, London: Economist Books
Harris, Nicola, *Basic Editing* (2 vols), London: Book House Training Centre
Hart's Rules for Compositors and Readers, Oxford: Oxford University Press (there is a planned combination of this title and the *Oxford Writers' Dictionary*)
Miller, Casey and Swift, Kate, *The Handbook of Non-sexist Writing for Writers, Editors and Speakers*, London: Women's Press

Dictionaries and Grammar

Bryson, B., *Penguin Dictionary of Troublesome Words* (2nd edn), Harmondsworth: Penguin
Carey, G. V., *Mind the Stop*, Harmondsworth: Penguin
Chambers English Dictionary, Edinburgh: Chambers
Chambers Thesaurus, Edinburgh: Chambers
The Concise Oxford Dictionary, Oxford: Oxford University Press
Fowler's Modern English Usage, Oxford: Oxford University Press
Oxford Dictionary for Scientific Writers and Editors, Oxford: Oxford University Press
The Oxford Spelling Dictionary, Oxford: Oxford University Press
The Oxford Writers' Dictionary, Oxford: Oxford University Press (there is a planned combination of this title and *Hart's Rules*)
Partridge, Eric (ed. J. Whitcut), *Usage and Abusage*, Harmondsworth: Penguin
Webster's New Collegiate Dictionary, Springfield, Mass.: Merriam-Webster (American dictionary)

General Reference

The Cambridge Factfinder, Cambridge: Cambridge University Press
Chambers Biographical Dictionary, Edinburgh: Chambers
The Macmillan World Almanac, London: Macmillan (published annually)
Pears Cyclopaedia, London: Pelham Books (published annually)
The Penguin Dictionary of Quotations, Harmondsworth: Penguin
Writers' and Artists' Yearbook, London: A. & C. Black (published annually)

Working with Computers

Dorner, J., *Writing on Disk*, Hatfield: John Taylor
Hewson, D., *Introduction to Desktop Publishing*, Hatfield: John Taylor
Miles, J., *Design for Desktop Publishing*, Hatfield: John Taylor
Taylor, J. and Heale, S., *Editing for Desktop Publishing*, Hatfield: John Taylor

Index

Note: E = Exercise; terms appearing
    only in the Glossary are not listed.

NOTES